THE SACRAMENT
PATH TO THE
[Purification, Illumination and Glorification]
(Lazar Puhalo)

SYNAXIS PRESS
BOX 18, DEWDNEY, BC
CANADA, V0M1H0

ISBN: 9798852683144
COPYRIGHT 2023

CONTENTS

INTENT
The Sacraments and the Process of Theosis

"The grace of the Sacraments is the grace of the Church, the grace of the Holy Spirit, the power of sanctification, by which her children are deified." (St Ambrose of Milan)

We understand the Church as a "Eucharistic society," and some other perfectly valid descriptions. I would like to look at it from another point of view, which in no way contradicts the standard descriptions of the Church, and of the eschatological aspect of the Divine Liturgy. The life of the Church is "sacramental" which means "to make something sacred." The sacraments of the Church are intended to bless, consecrate and sanctify our lives, leading us on the path to theosis. They sanctify every stage of our lives from baptism to the sacrament of Christian burial, and beyond to the Memorial Services for the departed.

We might suggest that the rather flat catechism description of the holy mysteries/sacraments is both insufficient and misleading. The sacraments are not merely an outward expression of invisible grace, as the scholastic catechisms say. There is nothing that redundant in the Orthodox Christian

1

liturgical cycle. Because of the nature of the Church and the actual role of the "royal priesthood" together with the ordained priesthood, we must suggest that the sacraments actually do accomplish something and are more than the mere outward appearance of some invisible action. The holy mysteries /sacraments accomplish the action as an act of synergy, a confluence of the grace of the Holy Spirit and the faith of the people of God. In the words of my mentor, Fr. John Romanides, "The Church sends no one to heaven or to hell. The purpose of the Church is to prepare people for their ultimate encounter with the love and glory of God." The path to theosis leads us through illumination and purification to glorification.[1]

In the absence of this consciousness, we see, on the one hand, the sacraments viewed as ethnic rituals and, on the other, as something magic accomplished by the priest saying the proper words. Faith and the participation of the whole household of God is a central element to the holy mysteries/sacraments. This is why it seems to me to be almost heretical to have a "by invitation only baptism" or a "by invitation only crowning of a marriage." These are all events in the household of God, and it seems almost blasphemous to say that some members of the household may be present but that other members of the household are to be excluded. There is no such thing as a "private" liturgical Divine service.

We would like to express an understanding of the sacraments of the Church as a confluence of grace and faith which serve in the process of Theosis. However else we might understand or define "the Church," we need to understand it in the context of the promise of Theosis and as the vector for that spiritual journey. The sacraments of the Church are elements of this path. Surely a principal ministry of the Church is to gather the community of the faithful into the "body of Christ" within the context of Theosis, not as a legal fiction but has a vital, life-bearing process.

The sacraments are more than liturgical formulas for blessing and consecration. Allow me to suggest that, most properly understood, the liturgical sacraments occur when the people of God – the Royal Priesthood – are gathered together in faith, led by the ordained priest, to call down the Holy Spirit to bless, to sanctify, to consecrate. I think that it will not be out of place to suggest that the sacraments are accomplished at this confluence of faith and grace, this synergy of the Divine energy of grace and the human energy of faith.

I would like to discuss the holy mysteries/sacraments in the context of the process of Theosis, and this process as a ministry of the Church. I will hope to make this aspect of the ministry of the Church to the faithful evident through a discussion of the greater meaning of the sacraments. I also want to demonstrate that the liturgical prayers in the sacraments are not simply "formulas," but are meant to teach and implant a spiritual understanding of the sacrament as blessing, consecration and purification by active presence of the Holy Spirit.

We are going to discuss the holy mysteries/sacraments in this context.

NOTES:
1. A theme that Romanides often spoke of.

ONE
BAPTISM/CHRISMATION
The Beginning of the Journey

Jesus answered, Verily, verily, I say unto thee, Except a man be born of water and of the Spirit, he cannot enter into the kingdom of God. That which is born of the flesh is flesh, and that which is born of the Spirit is spirit. (Jn.3:5-6)

The Saviour's resurrection was also a regeneration of the human nature "so that our Baptism in the likeness of the resurrection is our regeneration." (St Ambrose of Milan).[1]

Every journey has a beginning, a first step. Baptism is the illumination of the soul by the grace of the Spirit as it begins the journey of purification toward the destiny of glorification.

There is no "born again" without water. Jesus Christ did not say you must be born again of an emotional experience generated by a hyper-emotional pastor or preacher, but that you must be born again of water and the Spirit. This is a mystery of the

5

grace of the Holy Spirit. This mystery unfolds within the bosom of the Church, which is the body of Christ. The meaning of this mystery of holy baptism/chrismation[2] is inseparable from the revelation that redemption consists in ransom and theosis. Baptism cannot be understood as only symbolic, as an external symbol of something that has taken place mentally. It is an error to liken Christian baptism to the baptism of John, and Apostle Paul makes that abundantly clear.[3] The word "baptism" means simply "immersion," and it was practised among the Jews as a ritual purification; while John's baptism might not have been a prescribed *mikvah*,[4] it was certainly related. He himself makes the distinction that he baptised only with water but that Christ would also baptise with the Spirit.[5]

Christian baptism is an "initiation," but an initiation into what? If into the Church, let us remember that the Church is called "the body of Christ" and also the "pure virgin bride of Christ." Let us assert that both these descriptions indicate the Church as the vector of theosis, and that Baptism is "mile 0" the beginning of the path to that goal. All of the sacraments, as vectors of Divine Grace, are both nourishment for the journey and mileposts to mark the way.

WHAT DOES BAPTISM ACCOMPLISH?

"All of you that have been baptised into Christ have been robed in Christ." (Gal.3:27)[6]

Why the Baptismal font? Why do we immerse the person under the water when we baptize? In The first place because Christ was incarnate in the Virgin Mary by the descent of the Holy Spirit, born of a virgin. One is born again into the Body of Christ in a type and likeness of Christ's birth. With the descent of the Holy Spirit upon the Baptismal waters the Baptismal font becomes the womb of the Virgin Bride of Christ, the Church. So, we are born again in the womb of the Virgin by the descent of the Holy Spirit. In baptism, one is born again from the carnal into the spiritual, from the mortal into the eternal. This is also an image of the creation of life at which "the Spirit of God hovered over the water" (Gn.1:),[7] bringing forth life.

"That she/he may become a partaker of the death and resurrection of Christ."[8]

How are we made "partakers" of the death and resurrection of Christ? The mystery of redemption is clearly explained in the Epistle to the Hebrews. We are told that mankind was held in bondage to the fear of death by the one who has the power of death, namely the devil. The death and resurrection of Jesus Christ is the conquest of death.[9] We are ransomed from death itself and, therefore, the fear of death which held us in bondage.

Being ransomed from bondage, we are also redeemed from the power that Satan holds over us. Since the death and resurrection of Jesus Christ manifests His victory over these things, to be partakers of the death and resurrection of Christ is to participate in this ransom and redemption. Being immersed under the water in baptism and brought back up from the water is a type of the death and resurrection of Christ. We die to sin, to our alienation from God, we rise to Life. The service of baptism is designed to teach us this, not to teach us only but to make us actual participants, even as baptism and chrismation unite us to the body of Christ – the Church.

Why does a child begin to receive communion immediately after baptism/chrismation? A newly baptised child, forty days old, is a full member of the body of Christ, the Church. They grow up receiving communion by name each Sunday. Thus they realise that they "have a name" in the household of God, and thus an identity in the community. This is important in forming their bond with the body of Christ, the Church and the congregation around them.

What Are We Born Into?

It is well to recall at this point that the reason for the incarnation of Jesus Christ, His taking on the human nature while retaining his divine nature, has the purpose of ending the alienation between man and God by uniting the two in Himself and thus making it possible for each individual to be delivered from that alienation by becoming united to Christ.[10] This alienation from God is really the "sin of the world." We are told in Scripture that Christ came to take away the "sin of the world" (John 1:29). We are, first of all redeemed from our alienation from God.

Why do we call the Church the Body of Christ? The word *sin* in our "Orthodox language"[11] means to fall short of or miss the mark, to fall short of the goal, which is a reunion with the Divine, the healing of the fall. So, Christ came, in this Person, to reunite God and Man and overcome our alienation from God. The "body of Christ" consists of those who in faith have become united with Him, having "put on Christ" and having Him dwelling within them. Let us turn to the Scripture for a more complete explanation:

"Know you not that so many of us as were baptized *into Jesus Christ* were *baptized into His death*? therefore buried with Him [*syntaphemen, consupulti*] by Baptism into His death? that like as Christ was raised up from the dead by the glory of the Father, even so we also should walk in newness of life. For if we have been *planted together* [*symphytoi, conplantanti*] in the likeness of His death, we shall also rise in the likeness of His resurrection... For if we be dead with [*syn, cum*] Christ, we believe we shall also live with [*syn, cum*] Him." (Rm.6:3-5, 8).

Reborn or regenerated in Christ's Body through Baptism (Titus 3:5), the believer becomes a "partaker" of Christ's Sonship (Gal.4:4-7). He also become a "partaker of the Spirit" Who dwells in his body as in a temple, because the baptized are members or parts of His Body individually. The body of each becomes a "temple" and the Spirit dwells in him (1Cor.3:16). God lives in each Christian who acquires the Grace of fellowship (*koinonia, societas*) in the Spirit (Philippians 2:1).[12] "For as the body is one, and has many members, and all the members of that one body, although many, are one body; so also is Christ. For by one Spirit are we all baptized into one body... and have been all made to drink into one Spirit..." (1Cor.12:13).

The members of the Church, partake of Christ and His Spirit and, consequently, have become the adopted "children of God." "For as many as are led by the Spirit of God, they are the sons of God. You have received the Spirit of adoption, whereby we cry, 'Abba, Father'…we are the children of God; and if children, then heirs of God and *joint-heirs with* (*synkloronomoi, coheredes*) Christ; if, then, we *suffer with* Him (*sympaschomen, compatimur*), it is that we may also be *glorified with* (*syndoxathomen, conglorificemur*) Him" (Rm.8:14-17).

The alienation between God and Man has been abolished, and we are born into a new life in Christ, in which, by cooperation with the Holy Spirit, we are able to make our gradual assent toward glorification, toward "participation in the Divine Nature."

Baptism/Chrismation as Ordination

It seems somewhat dissonant and inconsistent to separate Chrismation and Baptism as two different sacraments. Baptism is not complete without Chrismation, and there can be no Chrismation without a Baptism. Perhaps the two have been separated just for the sake of creating the number seven because the Church of England and the Roman Catholic churches have a sacrament that they call "confirmation," which takes place when a person is 12 years of age, and it permits them, at that age, to receive their first communion. In the Orthodox Church, Baptism

11

and Chrismation are clearly combined, and an infant will receive Communion immediately, or as soon as possible, after Baptism/Chrismation. Even when someone converted to Orthodoxy is received through the ekonomia of Chrismation alone, it is clearly understood that the Chrismation is the completion of their previous baptism and supplies what was deficient in that baptism.

Chrismation is, in a manner of speaking, an anointing into the royal priesthood.[13] What does it mean to be a such a priest of the royal priesthood?

Under the law, only priests were allowed to partake of the Bread of the Presence and the things offered on the altar, that which was sacrificed in the temple.

What is now offered up on the altar except the bloodless sacrifice of the Body and Blood of Christ Jesus? We are made a royal priesthood first of all so that we may "partake of the things on the altar."[14]

The priest or bishop is fulfilling a higher priesthood, consecrated and ordained to serve Christ's Priesthood visibly for the sake of the faithful, offering the "Bloodless Sacrifice," calling for the Holy Spirit to *change* the Gifts, making them truly "the Bread of the very real Presence." This is an indefinable mystery in which we offer to Him that which we have received from Him, "Thine own of Thine own we offer unto Thee." The people, as a royal priesthood, are able to participate fully in the worship, in the offering itself, and to partake freely in the things offered on the altar. That is the result of our Chrismation at the end of our Baptism, it is our "ordination" into the royal priesthood.

Thus through Baptism and Chrismation, we have been reborn into the "Body of Christ," and having been born anew, we are babes. We must grow and mature with the help of the Holy Spirit. This is the aspect of the mystery that is so often missing when we think about or talk about the holy mystery of Baptism and Chrismation.

Water and the Spirit

Perhaps we should say something about the blessing and consecration of the baptismal water since Jesus Christ told us specifically to be born again of water and the Spirit. Why does one go under the water and come back out again, and why is water so significant here.

In the Creation narrative the Spirit of God hovered over the waters and life come forth from the waters. When God's people were being delivered from bondage, they passed through the Red Sea, and Apostle Paul tells us that the Hebrews were baptized in the Red Sea by Moses. This is why we refer to Baptism as "delivering us from the spiritual pharaoh."

When the Hebrews come to the undrinkable bitter waters of Mara, perishing from thirst, God instructs Moses to cast a two-branched tree limb (in the form of the Cross) into the bitter waters, and they become sweet and saves the perishing people. That is the first clear-cut blessing of the waters that we have. We imitate this blessing of the water both at a Baptism and at Theophany, the commemoration of the baptism of Christ. It is not a mere ritual, for the Holy Spirit is called down into the water to bless, consecrate and sanctify it.

ENDNOTES:

1. *The Mysteries*, III, 2 FOC
2. "Knowing only the baptism of John" (Acts 18:25).
3. See FN 1 above.
4. MIKVAH: Mikveh or mikvah is a bath used for the purpose of ritual immersion in Judaism to achieve ritual purity. Most forms of ritual impurity can be purified through immersion in any natural collection of water. However, some impurities, such as a zav, require "living water", such as rivers, springs or groundwater wells. In Aramaic or Hebrew, John the Baptizer would be literally, "John The Dipper."

5. Acts 19:3-5: And he said unto them, Unto what then were you baptized? And they said, Unto John's baptism. Then said Paul, John verily baptized with the baptism of repentance, saying unto the people, that they should believe on him which should come after him, that is, on Christ Jesus. When they heard this, they were baptized in the name of the Lord Jesus. See the command of Christ himself in the last verses in Matthew's Gospel.

6. ὅσοι γὰρ εἰς Χριστὸν ἐβαπτίσθητε, Χριστὸν ἐνεδύσασθε. "...For if Christ is the son of God, and you have put Him on, You have the Son in yourself and you are likened to Him, brought into one kinship and one form" (St John Chrysostom, P.G. 61:704, c656)

7. Man is about 60% water and 40%dust.

8. From the Litany of the Baptism.

9. Forasmuch then as the children are partakers of flesh and blood, He also Himself likewise took part of the same; that through death He might destroy him that had the power of death, that is, the devil; And deliver them who through fear of death were all their lifetime subject to bondage. (Hb.2:14-15)

10. "...For if Christ is the son of God, and you have put Him on, You have the Son in yourself and you are likened to Him, brought into one kinship and one form" (St John Chrysostom, P.G. 61:704, c656) 2

11. 'amartia (Gk) "to miss the mark, or fall short of the target."

12. Commonly translated "fellowship," *koinonia* or *societas* signifies much more than a community of interest or friendly relationship; it refers to organic unity of those who have been baptized into Christ. St Ambrose defines it as "a unity in the Faith by the bond of baptism, kinship in grace, by communion in the mysteries" (*De Off.* I, xxiii, 170). Thus, *koinonia* is a sharing of the divine-human life in the Body of Christ. The expressions "partaking in Christ" or "partaking of the Spirit" or, indeed, "partaking of the divine Nature" (See L.S. Thornton, *The Common Life in the Body of Christ*. London, 1944; and Odo Casel, *The Mystery of Christian Worship and other Writings*. Ed. by B. Neunheuser. London, 1962).

13. See 1 Peter 2:9 " you are a chosen race, a royal priesthood, a holy nation, a chosen people; that you should show forth the praises of Him who has called you out of darkness into his marvellous light." [cf Is.43:20; Ex.19:6, 23:22; Dt.7:6, 14:2; Is.43:21] "

14. And, of course, to "with one mouth and one heart" praise and glorify Him in the temple, and proclaim His gospel.

TWO
THE EUCHARIST
THE COMMUNION OF
THE BODY AND BLOOD OF CHRIST

The Eucharist is "the Sacrament of the eighth day"
(sacramentum octavi); St Gregory the Great
The Eucharist is "the medicine of immortality.
(St Ignatios the God-Bearer)

It is almost fearsome to speak about the great mystery of the holy Eucharist. One can only stand in awe and wonder before this great gift of grace that unites us with the creator and redeemer of the universe.

When the apostle says: *"Wherefore whosoever shall eat this bread, and drink this cup of the Lord, unworthily, shall be guilty of the body and blood of the Lord. But let a man examine himself, and so let him eat of that bread, and drink of that cup. For he that eateth and drinketh unworthily, eateth and drinketh damnation to himself, not discerning the Lord's body. For this cause many are weak and sickly among you, and many sleep," (1Cor.11:27-30)* he makes it abundantly clear that the Eucharist cannot be understood symbolically. No one becomes weak, sickly and dies from the mishandling of a mere symbol. The apostle is making it clear that we are partaking of the very body and blood of Christ.

16

Through the grace of the Holy Spirit which transforms the bread and wine into the very body and blood of Jesus Christ, we are partaking of that body in which our alienation from God has been healed; that body in which the power of death has been destroyed; that body which is seated at the right hand of the glory of God on our behalf. We are being healed and purified, and prepared for Theosis.

The Eucharist is the heart and soul of the Liturgy. It is a type of the wedding feast of the Heavenly Bridegroom and his earthly bride, the Church. Much of the Liturgy is preparation for Holy Communion, making us participants in the eschatological banquet. The Liturgy helps to prepare us for the great mystery of Holy Communion by bringing us to greater understanding of the nature of redemption. The Liturgy is filled with divine theology and this revelation helps in the process of purification of the faithful, provided we open our hearts to it and allow it to transform us. This inner transformation brings us ever closer to participation in the divine nature. This is the holy mystery and revelation *par excellence* that purifies us and brings us toward that "participation in the divine nature" that has been promised to us

According to the Scripture, Christ took leavened bread and broke it and distributed to His apostles. He took artos, not azymos for the mystical supper. In earlier times, especially in the Middle East, bread with leaven was referred to as "living bread," while bread without leaven was "dead bread." Christ was making it clear that He Himself is the living bread that descended from heaven. This is why we use leavened bread for the Holy Eucharist. If Christ used leavened bread even though it was the feast of unleavened bread, then He was unveiling a great revelation.

"Holy Communion:" let us think about what this means. Communion relates us to something other than ourselves. The incarnation of Jesus Christ brought the human nature back into communion with the divine nature. When we say that we are receiving the body and blood of Christ in Holy Communion, we mean that we are partaking of that incarnate nature of Christ which itself brought our humanity back into communion with God. It may be a mystery precisely why we commune of the body and blood of Christ, but the results of that communion are clear. Through the holy mystery of the Eucharist, we are brought into not only communion with the divine nature but with the whole body of Christ – the Church and all of those who constitute the Church, both the living and those who have departed this life. But let us pause on the purpose for the incarnation of God.

Christ was fully divine and became fully, completely human to redeem our nature from its alienation from God. When we receive Holy Communion, we are receiving of that deified human nature, which has been restored to full communion with the divine nature. This is and remains a great holy mystery, but it is one unveiled to us by Christ Himself and reiterated by Apostle Paul. We cannot suppose that we must become actually perfect and sinless in order to be redeemed by Christ Jesus; we must only strive toward that in the grace of the Holy Spirit. In the Eucharist, we are literally united with Christ and have Him dwelling in us in a literal sense. We become, therefore, partakers of the deified human nature and partake in that spiritual strengthening and power, that great grace that impels us on the path to the promised theosis.

Perhaps the concept of Holy Communion overwhelmed some people because they think of it in terms that are too carnal, and do not give any contemplation to the resurrected and deified Body of Christ.

As Orthodox Christians, we approach the Eucharist with knowledge and understanding of what we are about to partake of, and so we are called upon to approach "with fear of God, faith and love." No believer would dare to approach without preparation, and foremost in that preparation is to search our hearts and consciences and forgive everyone, remembering that Christ said that we would be forgiven to the degree that we forgive others. Even in the Lord's prayer, we ask to be forgiven as we have forgiven others. This is the first and foremost preparation for Holy Communion. During the whole of the Liturgy, however, we should be striving to absorb the revelation and meaning of the Divine Liturgy so that participation in the Liturgy is focussed on our preparation for Holy Communion.

Holy Communion brings us into communion not only with the heavenly kingdom, but with our brothers and sisters who are also receiving communion. When we partake of the Body and Blood of Christ we become, not simply symbolic brethren, but blood brothers and sisters through the blood of Christ Jesus. This fact should also help build in us that unselfish love that helps to purify us and drive out the divisive influence of Satan in our own lives and in the life of our community.

THREE
THE MYSTERY/SACRAMENT
OF ORDINATION
The Priesthood

Being a Spiritual Healer. Not a Prosecuting Attorney
Ministering to the "Royal Priesthood."
Lighting the Path to Theosis

The first duty of a priest is to know his congregation well enough that he can have a genuine compassionate love for them." (St Antony Khrapovitsky)

We usually date the formation of the Christian Church from Pentecost and the descent of the Holy Spirit. In the earliest days, while the apostles were still alive and teaching in the Christian community, they were also the "overseers" or bishops. The communities were small and were guided primarily by these teachers and their assistants, who were called "deacons." The word "deacon" means "one who serves."

As the number of communities increased and the assemblies became larger, some discord developed, often from outside the communities among those who opposed Christianity. The discord and confusion about the teachings of the faith multiplied also, and several forms of Christianity developed, causing more confusion and more discord. This necessitated a systematic development of teachers with authority in the church.

As the apostles began to die, they saw the necessity of ordaining replacements for themselves as teachers and overseers with authority. The deacons had already begun to function in the very earliest days of the Christian community being ordained by the leaders of the Church in Jerusalem to assist the apostles in serving the congregation, largely in charitable and communal activities.

The apostles ordained overseers, called bishops, to replace them as the teachers and guides and to preside at the liturgical services in each community. As the communities grew in number in each region, the task became heavier for the bishops, and presbyters were selected in each congregation to assist the bishops and represent them in teaching and presiding at the liturgical services.

The deacons, then, continued to assist the bishop's representative, the presbyter (priest) and continued to be responsible for the charitable work, visiting those in prisons and the ill. Their tasks included delivering Holy Communion to those who were in prisons or housebound and unable to attend the synaxis (gathering for prayer) of the faithful.

The continued expansion of the Church, coupled with the growing confusion and discord in the understanding of the Christian faith, necessitated a more structured organisation of the Christian community. In this way, the hierarchy and clergy of the Church developed as a necessity. Gradually, this also leads to some misunderstanding of the nature of the priesthood in the Congregations. That is what we wish to discuss here: the nature of the priesthood. We can readily understand the need for trained and informed teachers who were approved and had teaching authority in each congregation.

With prayer and the laying on of hands, the apostles called upon the grace of the Holy Spirit to sanctify their successors as leaders and teachers of the Church. The first successors of the apostles, in return, by the laying on of hands and the invocation of the Holy Spirit, consecrated their successors, and this has happened down to the present day so that our bishops have this "apostolic succession" passed from one generation to the next directly from the Holy Apostles.

In the ever-expanding Church, the burdens placed upon the bishops, who at one time presided over the Liturgy in every congregation, were no longer able to carry this out alone, and so they chose from among the approved elders in each congregation, assistants to help them and to preside in their place when they could not be personally present. With the laying on of hands of the Bishop, through the Grace of the Holy Spirit, these men were consecrated as "presbyters." And thus, the priesthood was extended from the bishops to the presbyters so that every congregation could be well served by a resident representative of the Bishop. The deacons continued to do what they had always done, to serve in any capacity to which the bishop assigned them. As they had assisted the Bishop, so they now assisted the presbyter, who was his delegate to the congregation.

The establishment of this hierarchy was necessary and logical, however, in the consecration of the ordained priests, we should never forget that the congregation of the faithful are all part of the "royal priesthood." The bishop or the ordained priest, when we serve the Liturgy, is actually serving the priesthood of Jesus Christ visibly for the sake of the faithful. The priesthood itself belongs only to Jesus Christ, but the bishops and presbyters are ordained to serve that priesthood in the Liturgy, visibly for the sake of the faithful, consecrating the holy gifts through the descent of the Holy Spirit to present Holy Communion to the faithful. This is why the priest exclaims, "Thine own of Thine Own we offer unto Thee."

This continuity from the holy apostles to the present is a significant aspect of the Orthodox Church. We will discuss the fact that the faithful are "a royal priesthood" when we talk about Holy Communion, although we had discussed it to some degree already when we spoke about Baptism and Chris-mation.

We should understand that the role of the Bishop and presbyter in serving the priesthood of Jesus Christ visibly in the church, is primarily for the consecration of Holy Communion and presiding at the Liturgy, to minister to the faithful in the process of Theosis leading the congregation in the ongoing process of consecration, sanctifying and blessing in all of the Sacraments. The faithful, gathered together in faith, led by the ordained bishop or presbyter, call on the grace of the Holy Spirit to bless, to consecrate and to sanctify the people of God in this process toward the great grace of our ultimate Theosis; our participation in the Divine Nature. The priesthood itself, which is vested in the Bishop and the presbyters is a visible revelation of the ever-present High Priesthood of Jesus Christ. Since they are serving visibly the priesthood of Christ, they alone can consecrate the Holy Gifts, calling upon the Holy Spirit to change them into the presence of the body and blood of Jesus Christ.

If we examine the prayers read by the priest as he vests for the Liturgy, we gain a deeper understanding of the priesthood itself.

As the priest puts on the first robe, the sticharion, he says the following: "Blessed is our God who has robed me with a robe of salvation. He has placed upon my head the crown of precious stones as a bridegroom."

The priest, and the entire congregation, are clothed in the Holy Spirit as with a robe of salvation, but the priest is also crowned as a bridegroom. The Bridegroom of the Church is Jesus Christ and the priesthood belongs only to Jesus Christ, our great High Priest. To say that the priest is crowned as a bridegroom indicates that he is serving the priesthood of Jesus Christ visibly for the sake of the faithful. The robe represents the baptismal robe given to the faithful at their baptism. The rest of the vestments are built up from that foundation.

The "bridegroom crown" indicates the nature of his priesthood and his relationship to that service. The priest should always remember that he does not so much possess the priesthood as the priesthood possesses him and that, ultimately, it is Christ's Priesthood, for it is He Who both offers and is offered.

A most significant prayer is the one for the putting on of the Epitrachelion. "Blessed is our God who has poured forth grace upon his priest like the oil of myrrh that runs down upon the beard of Aaron, down to the fringe of his raiment." This vestment must be worn whenever the priest is leading in prayer or any divine service. The epitrachelion reveals the shield of divine grace, which permits the priest to stand where no man has a right to stand and serve things that no man is worthy to serve. Without the shield of divine grace, he would be spiritually burned and destroyed by serving the priesthood on behalf of Christ.

With the belt [zonos], the priest prays to be girt with the strength of grace so that his service may be blameless, which can only be so by grace.

With the prayer for the felonion [or sakkos for a bishop], the priest asks God to clothe him in righteousness since he has no righteousness of his own but must receive it by grace through the Holy Spirit in order to be able to serve the ineffable mystery of the bloodless sacrifice. With this prayer, he acknowledges that only through divine grace can we be made ritually pure and able to serve before the altar, to serve the dread mystery.

Placing the cuff on the right hand, we acknowledge with the prayer that Christ has defeated our adversary on our behalf. As we place the cuff on the left hand, we ask for understanding that we may comprehend the law of the Lord.

We must take these vesting prayers seriously and not think of them as mere formulas or formalities. The vesting prayers have meaning, and we should take this meaning to heart and understand what we are saying as we proclaim these prayers and robe ourselves in the liturgical vestments.

The vestments are not intended to elevate us above the people but rather to remind us of our unworthiness and that only through the grace of the Holy Spirit are we made worthy to serve before the altar and to lead the people of God in prayer and worship.

The Royal Priesthood

Having spoken about the ordained priesthood of the Church, it is necessary to speak about the "royal priesthood." Apostle Peter, in his epistle, refers to the whole body of Christian people as a "Royal Priesthood." We spoke about this briefly and the section on the Mystery of Baptism, but we should say something about it here, also. According to the liturgical law in the Old Testament, only priests could partake of the things offered on the altar. There was a special reference to the "bread of the presence," which was always kept on a small table near the Holy of Holies. This, too, was to be consumed only by priests, and this is the key to understanding what is meant by "the Royal priesthood." The faithful, having been baptised and chrismated with the seal of the gift of the Holy Spirit, constitute a special priesthood able to receive of the things offered on the altar. We may think of the holy gifts which are set up on the altar to be consecrated as the bread of the presence of Jesus Christ.

The people are also a royal priesthood because they serve in the temple as the ordained priest served in the altar, which is the holy of holies in the Orthodox Christian temple. The Fathers remind us that the ordained priest does not serve the Holy Eucharist alone, saying:. "The offering of the Eucharist again is common: for neither doth he [the ordained priest] give thanks alone, but also all the people. For having first heard their voices, when they assent that it is 'meet and right' to do so, then he begins the thanksgiving." (St John Chrysostom, *Homily 18, on 2nd Corinthians,* 4th century.)

"When all make their profession of the divine faith together, they anticipate the mystical thanksgiving [Eucharist]...In making that thanksgiving, the worthy confirm their gratitude for God's kindness, having no other way to reciprocate God's infinite blessings" (St Maximos the Confessor, *The Mystagogia, 34:31* 7th century).

"The priest says: 'Let us give thanks unto the Lord.' The people affirm: 'It is meet and right'..." (St Germanos of Constantinople, *Commentary on the Divine Liturgy,* 41. 8th century).

"The celebrant addresses to God this act of thanksgiving: 'Let us give thanks unto the Lord.' The faithful give their consent, saying, 'It is meet and right'." (Nicholas Kavasilas, *Commentary on the*

Divine Liturgy, Ch.26. 14th century).

The ordained priests serve not only God, but they also serve the "royal priesthood," the faithful. By leading in the holy mysteries/sacraments, and by distributing Holy Communion, the body and blood of Christ Jesus, they serve in the journey toward Theosis of the whole congregation of the people of God.

CHRIST OUR GREAT HIGH PRIEST
AND SAVIOUR

FOUR
CONFESSION
THE MYSTERY OF PEACE
AND RECONCILIATION

Ultimately, the Mystery of Confession is an element in the process of the purification of our conscience on the path toward Theosis. Taking responsibility for our sins and spiritual shortcomings and coming to sincere repentance helps keep us on that path toward the glorious destiny to which God has called us through Jesus Christ and with the help and guidance of the Holy Spirit.

Confession is therapeutic and is a manifestation of the Church as a spiritual hospital. Our conscience is our sternest judge. An unpeaceful conscience is a spiritual illness and can be more tormenting than physical pain It can even lead to emotional and mental illness and even to physical illness.

The sacrament of confession has been given to us to help heal an unpeaceful conscience and aid in our spiritual struggle. If we confess before an experienced and compassionate priest, this can heal our confusion, cleanse our conscience and strengthen our struggle against our passions.

At times we may feel estranged from God, but we also have times when we feel estranged from our community and even feel estrangement from our own selves. Confession is intended to help us through such times and reconcile us with God, our community, and our own selves. This is psychologically beneficial. A skilful priest can help us take responsibility for our actions and thoughts in a positive manner, comfort us in our distress, and apply those healing actions and mental dispositions which can make us feel whole and restore our peace of mind.

A primary function of Confession is the act of taking responsibility for one's actions and for those negative thoughts that one allows to occupy one's mind. Accepting and acknowledging one's responsibility is the first step in the process of moral healing and reconciliation, first of all with oneself, cleansing your conscience and bringing it to peace.

Confession is never about punishment. Punishment and forgiveness are mutually exclusive. If you are punished, you are not forgiven, and if you are forgiven, there can be no punishment. We need to realise this because we often punish ourselves, sometimes ruthlessly, and this is destructive. It is far better to be guided in taking responsibility without despair. If the one to whom we are confessing feels that we need to take some action that will help to heal our conscience, make it easier for us to accept forgiveness, and also to forgive ourselves through repentance, these actions are not for the sake of punishment, but are spiritually and mentally therapeutical.

For example, if we are told to make some number of prostrations, with prayer, then we might understand a prostration as an image of the death and resurrection of Christ. We should image ourselves as dying to sin and rising to life as we make each prostration and rise up again. Such physical actions that we take when necessary help us in the process of repentance and also help us to be open to accepting forgiveness and also forgiving ourselves. This can be very powerful in helping us to come to peace and reconciliation.

An important aspect of the healing process is accepting the forgiveness that comes in response to sincere repentance and letting go of the guilt that preceded the repentance. Having received God's forgiveness and the reconciliation with the body of Christ that comes with it, one must readily forgive oneself and not cling to guilt or shame. While we struggle against judging others, we must also realise that judging ourselves too harshly can also be spiritually destructive and can actually lead to unhealthy self-focus. The self-pity that can ultimately arise from this is one of the most destructive spiritual conditions we can develop. Holding on to guilt and shame after one has repented can lead to self-pity and psychological, sometimes physical, illness. When one has received forgiveness from God, it is irrational not to accept that forgiveness completely and forgive oneself with the resolve of truly striving to correct our life.

The spiritual healing and reassurance we receive in confession can lift a heavy burden from our souls and help keep us on the path of spiritual growth toward unity with God, reassuring us of His love just as the prodigal son was assured of the father's compassion. This is why many people feel relieved of heavy burdens following Confession.

Ultimately, the Mystery of Confession is an element in the process of the purification of our conscience on the path toward *Theosis*. Taking responsibility for our sins and spiritual shortcomings and coming to sincere repentance helps keep us on that path toward the glorious destiny to which God has called us through Jesus Christ and with the help and guidance of the Holy Spirit.

FIVE
THE SACRAMENT OF ANOINTING

"Is any among you sick? Let him call for the presbyters of the church to anoint him..." (Js.5:14)

The anointing service should not be thought of as being only for physical illness. It has a genuine therapeutic value for spiritual illness or addictions. The anointing service should be part of one's treatment for all these kinds of illnesses since the anointing is for the "healing of soul and body." Even when physical illness or addiction, which is a spiritual illness, is being treated by other means, the anointing service should be a part of our treatment. Psychologically, it is therapeutic and is helpful in placing our frame of mind in a positive and peaceful disposition, and such a disposition always promotes healing.

Certainly, we receive divine grace for healing in the anointing service, but it also strengthens us emotionally and mentally to endure with patience whatever is set before us. We should not allow any medical or psychiatric treatment to be interrupted by the anointing service but should continue with our medical treatment. The same must be said for addictions. If one is a member of Narcotics Anonymous, for example, one should continue to participate in the meetings even after having been free of narcotics for years.

When the anointing service is served in the parish community, usually at the end of a Liturgy, we should understand the healing service as applying to the entire community. When serving this service in the church, especially at the end of a Liturgy, we should remind the community that the services are for the healing of the community itself, and we should pay attention to any stresses, destabilisation, or upsets that may afflict the community and pray especially for the healing of those demonic temptations. We should also direct the service toward healing the anxieties, enmities, malice or hatred afflicting any member of the congregation who is suffering from those destructive passions.

Whenever we serve the Divine Liturgy and hear the refrain, "Lord have mercy!" repeated over and over again, let us recall that in Greek, the word for "mercy" and the olive oil we use for anointing both have the same root: ελαιόλαδο and έλεος –Kiri eleison. In my mind, I hear the refrain "Lord have mercy" as "Lord anoint me." Lord, anoint my troubled soul and bring it to peace. Lord, anoint my troubled mind and purge it of all judgmentalness, enmity, envy and malice and bring my mind to peace." Lord, anoint my conscience and help my struggle to purify it. Lord, anoint my doubts and uncertainties and bring me to the fullness of Faith. Lord, help me to keep my focus on the "the prize of the high calling of God in Christ Jesus" (Phil.3:14), " and run with patience the race that is set before me" (Hb.12:1) that by grace I might acquire that crown and become a "partaker of the divine nature" (2Pt.1:4).

SIX
THE SACRAMENT OF
HOLY WATER
AND THE BLESSING OF HOMES
Sanctifying the daily lives of the faithful

When the Hebrews came to the undrinkable bitter waters of Mara, perishing from thirst, God instructs Moses to cast a two-branched tree limb (in the form of the Cross) into the bitter waters, and they become sweet and saved the perishing people. That is the first clear-cut blessing of the waters that we have. We imitate this blessing of the water both at a Baptism and at Theophany, the commemoration of the baptism of Christ

We imitate this blessing of the water at Mara both at a Baptism and at Theophany, the commemoration of the baptism of Christ. It is not a mere ritual, for the Holy Spirit is called down into the water to bless, consecrate and sanctify it.

After the blessing of the water at Theophany, the priest takes the holy water to the homes of the faithful and blesses them, taking the sanctity of the temple into every dwelling, beginning the blessing at the icon corner, which is the spiritual heart of every Orthodox Christian home.

The Orthodox Church, through her sacraments,

blesses and sanctifies every part of our lives, every step from baptism to death. All of these sacraments, this blessing and sanctification leads us on the path toward the promised Theosis. We should understand this as the actual meaning of the sacraments/holy mysteries of the Holy Church.

SEVEN
THE SACRAMENT
OF MARRIAGE[1]
The Meaning of Marriage
Marriage as Revelation and Prophecy

"Shall I tell you how marriage is also a mystery of the Church? Christ came into the Church, and She was made of Him, and He united with Her in spiritual intercourse ... So marriage is a type of the presence of Christ" *(St John Chrysostom, Homily on Ephesians).*

This is not a concept which is new to Apostle Paul or Chrysostom. The prophets of the Old Testament regularly used the terminology of spousal relationship to describe the covenant between God and Israel. Apostle Paul was reaffirming that understanding of the new covenant which was not intended as a legal agreement or a treaty, but a spousal relationship; a relationship that helps to heal our selfish love and make us capable of genuine unselfish love.

Both the prophets and the apostles see marriage as revealing the nature of the covenant relationship between God and humanity. The covenant is not a legalistic treaty between God and humanity but a spousal relationship in which a mutual love and the fidelity of marriage is the dynamic.

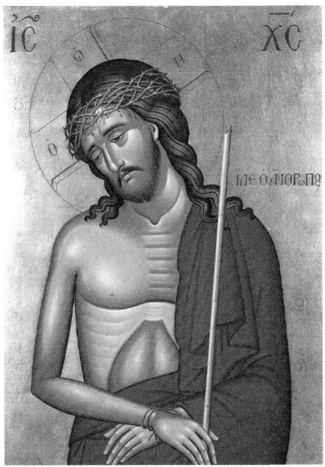

Christ the "Bridegroom of the Church"
The crown of thorns was His wedding crown

We refer marriage to prophecy because married couples bear that revelation and project it in time. That is the higher spiritual vocation of marriage with the revelation being the nature of the covenant. The prophecy is in bearing that revelation and projecting it in time. It is not that every married couple can actually fulfil their role as a "type" of that revelation, but that the meaning is expressed in the nature of Orthodox Christian marriage. The struggle of marriage is to ascend toward fulfilling that revelation through the prophetic vocation of marriage. The growth toward pure love, unselfish love and the struggle against the ego, which is required in order to accomplish that, is an aspect of the prophetic vocation of the spousal relationship. We see marriage as the union of two people to mutually work out their salvation. The challenge to the undisciplined ego is an example of how husband and wife help each other in the struggle since egotism is a mark and result of the fall of mankind.

Beyond being bearers of that revelation and projecting it, striving to live it, the struggle to ascend in unselfish love is part of the process of purification, an image of the ascent toward Theosis. This is why both marriage and our children are elements in the process of our salvation: the fact that they elicit the manifestation of unselfish love in us and lead us to a growth in that unselfish love. Pure unselfish love is a manner of bearing our cross since Christ on the Cross is the manifestation of unfathomable, pure unselfish love. Marriage and family is a path toward that kind of love. The ascent in that type of love is an aspect of the journey toward Theosis.

This role of marriage as revelation of the meaning of the Covenant constitutes a higher spiritual dimension of the meaning of marriage. It must be understood as a vector of that meaning if, as Paul says, marriage is a type and likeness of Christ and the Church. We refer to the married couple as "prophetic" because the prophets are the guardians and teachers of the revelation. In this regard it is notable that during the crowning of marriage in the Orthodox Church, the couple are blessed in the name of the Old Testament prophetic couples.

The revelation through marriage of the meaning of the covenant certainly makes it a sacrament of the Church, but there is another dimension which makes a sacramental step toward Theosis.

Marriage and the Path to Theosis

"....The uncreated glory that belongs to Christ by nature from His Father is Paradise to those whose egocentric and selfish love has been cured and transformed into unselfish love. The same glory, however, is eternal, uncreated fire and perdition for those who elect to remain unhealed in their selfishness." (Fr John Romanides)

The struggle to acquire unselfish love is a dominant aspect of our Orthodox Christian life, and of our salvation. When we enter into a marriage based on love, the healing of our self-love, our egotism, begins to be modified through the experience of mutual love that manifests itself in unselfish love. Nothing can create unselfish love in us as much as having children. Most parents have genuinely unselfish love for their children to the degree that some parents would certainly give their own lives for the sake of their children. This growth in unselfish love, which moderates egotism and self-focus, is a major aspect of our Orthodox Christian spiritual life and is clearly an aspect of the path toward Theosis, toward participation in the divine nature, which is the calling and destiny of all faithful believers. Romanides has expressed this so clearly and the above quote in which he also describes the true nature of heaven and hell.

44

We should constantly be reminding our Orthodox Christian people that marriage is a sacrament, first of all, because it reflects the true meaning of the covenant relationship between God and His people and secondly, because it should be a path toward the acquisition of and growth in, unselfish love.

The Incarnation of the Son of God, Jesus Christ, is a manifestation of God's unselfish co-suffering love for mankind. This is the healing power in the ministry of Christ. Being both fully God and fully man removed the alienation between the divine nature and the human nature as the major aspect of our redemption. Marriage unites two opposites into one, making them "one flesh," just as Jesus Christ calls us all together into one "body of Christ," recapitulating our human nature.

One could make several emotional, even maudlin, comments about marriage. Marriage is a difficult struggle, even more difficult than the monastic struggle. There are many ups and downs and pitfalls in marriage and we should not be too hyperbolic in describing it and trying to say too many saccharine things about it. It is a challenge. The struggle against the ego and toward unselfish love is a difficult path, but it is the calling of Orthodox Christian people, not only in marriage but in parish life. Please see the appendix for the more "mundane" implications marriage.

The unselfish love that we develop for one another is a pale shadow of the unselfish love that enthroned Jesus Christ on the Cross for our ransom and redemption. Marriage and, if we are so blessed, children are a clear path toward developing such unselfish love and, therefore a path of salvation, a path toward the high calling that is set before us that we may become participants in the Divine nature; this and the fact that it reveals the nature of the covenant, is what makes marriage a sacrament.

NOTES:

1. Marriage was not considered a sacrament in the Latin West until the 12 hundreds. It was strongly debated at the time that it was included partly because marriage is a universal phenomenon and partly because Augustin had said that marriage is a venial sin cloaked in the guise of respectability for the sake of procreation. According to Kurgansky, it was not designated as a sacrament in Russia until the 16 hundreds although it was always treated as one, and the Orthodox Church has never had a doctrine of "seven sacraments." It is as a type of the covenant, both Old Testament and New Testament, that we approach the sacramental nature of it here in this work. In some Christian traditions, marriage is only a ritual that allows people to have legitimate sexual relations.

TWO OTHER DIVINE SERVICES THAT BIND HEAVEN AND EARTH TOGETHER

1
MYSTERY OF CHRISTIAN BURIAL

"And this is the reason for the prayers, psalms and glorifications of God [at burial services]: so that you not weep and lament, but rather give thanks to God Who has taken him." (St John Chrysostom)[1]

We had mentioned before that the Orthodox Christian Church does not doctrinally have a limited number of sacraments. However, for the sake of ecumenism it seems that we have become used to limiting them to the number seven as our Roman Catholic and Anglican brethren do. It is clearly arbitrary not to consider the Rite of Christian Burial to be a Sacrament. The Orthodox Church sanctifies every step of our lives, from the baptismal font to the grave, with Orthodox Christian Sacraments. If the funeral service is not a Sacrament, then we should be free to serve it for anyone, Orthodox or not.

Nevertheless, let us explore the funeral/ burial

47

service and see what it does and what it does not mean, because, as with many of the prayers and divine services mythologies, strange, even lugubrious, ideas have appeared concerning the funeral and memorial services. Some of these mythologies actually slander God and portray Him as being as unmerciful, vengeful and vindictive as Satan.

The rite of Christian burial, the Orthodox Christian funeral service, is part of the long chain of blessing and sanctification that is an integral part of the life of the Church. It accents the role of the Church in preparing the faithful for their encounter with the glory and love of Jesus Christ. Remember that the vocation of the Church is not to send anyone to heaven or to hell, but to prepare the faithful for that ultimate encounter with the glory and love of Jesus Christ, which actually constitutes both the partial and the last judgment.

The prayers of the funeral service, like the prayers of the memorial services that follow it, do not concern only the person who has fallen asleep but are an aspect of the spiritual education and purification of those who remain. To the degree that these services are offered in genuine love, they do serve for our purification since purification is a growth in unselfish love. As we read the holy fathers comments on the services, we find that they are "pedagogical."

This means that they deeply instruct us both spiritually and mentally, deepening our relationship with Christ by expanding our spiritual understanding.

Especially significant are the words of Saint Dionysios[2] in his complete theological exposition, *"Concerning Things Performed Over Those Fallen Asleep*:

"...now the prayer beseeches the supremely Divine Goodness to remit to the person fallen asleep all the failings committed by reason of human infirmity, and to transfer him in the light [or, light-filled] land of the living (Ps.56:14; 116:9) into the bosom of Abraham (Lk.16: 22) and Isaak and Jacob; in a place where grief and sorrow and sighing are no more. It is, I think, evident then, that these, the rewards of the pious are most blessed...

"But you may, perhaps, say that these things are indeed correctly affirmed by us, but want to know for what reason the hierarch beseeches the supremely Divine Goodness for the remission of the sins committed by the person fallen asleep, and [that he may receive] his most glorious inheritance....For, if everyone shall receive, by the divine justice, equivalent to what he has done in the present life, whether it be good or otherwise, and the person fallen asleep has finished his own activities in this present life, from what prayer offered by the hierarch will he be transferred to another inheritance than that due to and equivalent for his life here?

"Now, well do I know, following the Scriptures, that each one will have the inheritance equivalent; for the Lord says, he has closed respecting him, `and each one shall receive the things done in his body according to that [which] he has done, whether it be good or bad' (2Cor.5:10). Yes, the sure Traditions of the Scripture teach us that the prayers even of the just avail only for those who are worthy of pious prayers, during this present life, by no means after death. What, in truth did Saul gain from Samuel? (1Sm. 16:1). And what did the intercessions of the prophet profit the people of the Hebrews? (Jer.7:15-16)

"Now with reference to the prayer mentioned, which the hierarch prays over the person fallen asleep. .. the holy hierarch...has learned then, from the God transmitted Scriptures, that to those who have passed their life piously, the most bright and divine life is given in return (1Jn.5:16), according to their due...the divine love overlooking, through its goodness, the stains which have come to them through human infirmity, since no-one, as the Scripture says, is free of blemish (Jb.14:4).

"Now, the hierarch knew that these things have been promised by the infallible Scriptures; and he asks that these things may come to pass, and that the righteous returns be given to those who lived piously...and while knowing that the promises will be unfailing, he makes known clearly to those present that the things asked by him according to the holy law, will be entirely realized for those who have been perfected in a holy life. For the hierarch... would never seek things which were not pleasing to the Almighty God, and divinely promised to be given by him" (Apostolic Constitutions.8:43).

We had cited these words of Chrysostom

earlier: "And this is the reason for the prayers, psalms and glorifications of God [at burial services]: so that you not weep and lament, but rather give thanks to God Who has taken him."[3]

As we saw above, according to our Saint Dionysios, the prayers and commemoration for the reposed serve primarily to educate the faithful regarding the promises given to those who struggle for salvation and the opposite end of those who are faithless. He declares that the things we ask on behalf of the reposed are only proclamations of what they are going to receive through His mercy, because God has already promised them, and so far from Him requiring our prayers in order for Him be merciful, He readily, without our prompting, overlooks those sins and stains the faithful died with. He does not keep some kind of "scorecard" but knows the heart and the volition and the disposition of the soul, and this he "accounts to us for righteousness" on account of Christ. Remember that it is our own conscience that renders the judgement.

Recall also that the prayers of the funeral service are there to reaffirm our own spiritual understanding and encourage us in our struggle for the purification of our own consciences. This is an integral part of the sacramental life of the Orthodox Church.

ENDNOTES:

1. P.G.96:33A.

2. We are aware that the words of Saint Dionysios "the Areopagite" I published as "pseudo-Dionysios, and that they were published not before the fourth century. However, they have considerable authority in the Orthodox Church and his words about the funeral service are fully in accord with the Tradition and theology of the Orthodox faith. His works were used extensively by Saint Gregory Palamas and others as completely authoritative.

3. P.G.96:33A.

2
MEMORIALS
FOR THE DEPARTED

"For I am persuaded that neither death nor life, nor angels nor principalities nor powers nor things present nor things to come, nor height nor depth nor any other creature, shall be able to separate us from the love of God which is in Christ Jesus our Lord." (Rm.8:38-39.)

Death, the Apostle says, cannot separate us from the love of our Saviour. And another time he says, "To live is Christ and to die is gain...for I am torn between the two, having a desire to depart and to be with Christ, which is far better" (Phil.1:21-23).

The memorial services are another example of the vocation of the Church is a spiritual hospital. The memorial services for the third, ninth and fortieth day and first anniversary of a person's demise are really "stepping away from grief rituals" for those who have lost a loved one. This is part of the psychological healing that we receive through the Church.

When we offer a memorial service from love for the departed, since God is love no act of love goes unfulfilled. By serving memorial services for the departed, we also confess the close connection between heaven and the Church on earth. The memorial services are served not only for the departed, but as a comfort and consolation for those whom they have left behind.

While there have been several twisted and grotesque mythologies about the purpose of the services, their meaning is really simple and straightforward and healing. The symbolic meaning for serving these memorial services on the third, ninth and fortieth days after a person's repose is a comforting revelation.

We are told by the holy fathers and sacred tradition that we serve a memorial service on the third day because Christ rose from the dead on the third day, assuring us that we likewise will rise. The service on the ninth day informs us that since the soul cannot receive its recompense without the body, it is kept by the nine orders of holy angels. Saint Symeon of Thessaloniki, the great liturgist, tells us that the ninth-day commemoration service is for the sake of the living, those grieving for a departed person. It should be obvious what the fortieth-day service actually means. Christ ascended into heaven, both body and soul together, on the fortieth day after his Resurrection. And this promises us that the departed will also ascend both body and soul together after their resurrection.

Traditionally, the first anniversary of a departed

spouse allows the surviving spouse to remarry without any feelings of betrayal or unfaithfulness to the departed spouse. Psychologically, this gives a person "permission" to continue with their life without any negative feelings.

We have seen some dark and lugubrious mythological reasons given for these memorial services, the most frequently cited ones taken from the pagan Egyptian "Book of the Dead," the embalming texts of Pharaonic Egypt. Let us examine the actual doctrinal treatments of these memorial days from actual Orthodox Christian sources rather than some allegorical mythology, often even cited and repeated by Orthodox Christian writers and leaders. The words of Chrysostom cited above about the funeral prayers certainly apply:

"And this is the reason for the prayers, psalms and glorifications of God [at burial services]: so that you not weep and lament, but rather give thanks to God Who has taken him."[1]

How do the memorial services unite heaven and earth?

If the soul who has fallen asleep is with Christ, could it not be also with His Body, the Church? For, if the Apostle says that none of these things, not even death, can separate us from Christ, he says as well that they cannot separate us from the Church.

It is manifest, therefore, that those who do not commemorate and offer prayers on behalf of the reposed do not recognize Christ's victory over death, that death is set at naught, that the mutual love of those who live in and by Christ is in no wise severed or broken by this defeated and shattered enemy, for, "Whether we live, we live unto the Lord; and whether we die, we die unto the Lord: whether we live therefore, or die, we are the Lord's" (Rm.14:8).

These things, then, are abundantly clear: that we are bound by bonds of undefeatable love that is of Christ and the Holy Spirit, and that we pray for one another, not as though at death we passed into annihilation and non-existence, but as knowing that those who have fallen asleep are among the living and are still "members in particular of the body of Christ" (1Cor.12:27). And the very fact that we pray for the reposed is an active confession of our faith in the victory of Christ and our sure hope in the resurrection.

Although the reasons for our prayers and commemorations of those who have fallen asleep are so simple and have been set forth so clearly from the earliest times, through vain curiosity and speculation, a great fog of misunderstanding and confusion has arisen around this subject. The speculations of men have come to be considered as some kind of holy tradition. And although these traditions of men contradict the pure, simple doctrine of the fathers, because of the prejudice of habit, they have come to be defended as doctrines. It must be said that, for the most part, these customs (they ought not to be called traditions at all) have come to us from Gnostic philosophies and pagan cultures.

If we compare these two, the precise theological teachings of the fathers and the various, sometimes ancient, mythologies, allegories and tales, we are struck by the immensity of the difference. While most of these, basically Gnostic, tales and doctrines are complex, labyrinthine, morbid and tediously legalistic, exalting the power of demons and rendering God cold, remote and almost indifferent, the patristic theological teachings are simple, completely characteristic of the Scripture and firmly based in the love of God and the clear fact that Christ is the only judge that we will ever face. This is of the greatest significance: that the mythological teachings and doctrines are based on the fear of demons and a certain remoteness of God, while the patristic theological teachings are clearly rooted in the sure knowledge of the closeness, love and mercy of our Lord Jesus Christ.

Before setting forth the patristic theological teachings on the prayers and commemoration of those who have fallen asleep, let us present an outline of the points we wish to make:

[1] We will present the exact words of the holy fathers about the third, ninth and fortieth-day commemorations and the memorial service held on the first anniversary of a person's repose. We must point out that these services are "stepping away from grief" rituals for the sake of those who are grieving. St. John Chrysostom says: "And this is the reason for the prayers, psalms and glorifications of God [at burial and memorial services]: so that you not weep and lament, but rather give thanks to God Who has taken him." It was the custom that, after the one-year service, a widow or widower could remarry without feeling remorse.

[2] The prayers and commemorations for the reposed are acts of love and confessions of faith, not bribes to God, means of satisfying His "need for vengeance," nor appeasements to demons.

[3] While the reposed benefit greatly from our prayers and commemorations, this benefit is in the form of a spiritual increase, an increase in their joy and in the mutual exchange of co-suffering love. It is not true that our prayers are offered as appeasements to Satan, to teach God how to be merciful, to obtain repose for the soul, to bribe the soul's way through some demonic turnpike, to "pay off the demons" or any other such thing.

[4] The prayers for the reposed do not change the condition, the "inheritance" of the reposed, or obtain for them anything which God will not give them even without our poor prayers. For, when we ask anything on behalf of the reposed, we ask only what God has already promised. Our prayers are not bailiffs who force God to pay His promises or instructors which shame Him into mercy. They are expressions of our faith in God's promises and expressions of our mutual love.

[5] The prayers and commemorations for the reposed, while they fulfil the calling of love, serve primarily to instruct the living. For, in the prayers, we often mention not only the hope of the faithful but at the same time, we are being reminded of our own mortality and the day of our own death in order to encourage our own repentance.

When we see what the prayers and commemorations for the reposed do mean, we shall also understand what they do not mean. We mentioned that we were going to turn to the "precise patristic theological statements" on the subject.

What are the benefits of these prayers and commemorations, then? Our holy, apostolic father Dionysios, in a most complete theological exposition, *"Concerning Things Performed Over Those Fallen Asleep,"* replies:

"..now the prayer beseeches the supremely

Divine Goodness to remit to the person fallen asleep all the failings committed by reason of human infirmity, and to transfer him in the light [or, light-filled] land of the living (Ps. 56; 13; 116:9) into the bosom of Abraham (Lk.16: 22) and Isaak and Jacob; in a place where grief and sorrow and sighing are no more. It is, I think, evident then, that these, the rewards of the pious, are most blessed...

"But you may, perhaps, say that these things are indeed correctly affirmed by us, but want to know for what reason the hierarch beseeches the supremely Divine Goodness for the remission of the sins committed by the person fallen asleep, and [that he may receive] his most glorious inheritance....For, if everyone shall receive, by the divine justice, equivalent to what he has done in the present life, whether it be good or otherwise, and the person fallen asleep has finished his own activities in this present life, from what prayer offered by the hierarch will he be transferred to another inheritance than that due to and equivalent for his life here?

St Epiphanios of Cyprus also gives us a very clear and definite theological statement on this subject. Here, he is specifically refuting a certain heresy that denied prayers and commemorations for the reposed. Here, he is drawing forth from the whole Tradition and Conscience of the Church. Aerios was questioning prayers for the reposed:

"Then he [Aerios] asks, `for what reason do you commemorate the names of the dead after their death? If a living person prays or gives out alms, what profit will this be to a dead person? But if the prayer of those here could really profit those yonder, let no man be pious, let no man do good! Rather let him gain some friends by any means whatever, and persuading them with money or having them simply as friends at the time of his death, they shall pray for him, lest he suffer anything yonder, or any grave sin he has committed be required of him'."

Now this question is not without merit and the speaker makes a perfectly valid point, for this is exactly the absurdity the Latins fell into at an early date. Saint Epiphanios responds directly to this question, and we may do well to look at some other responses to such questions. St Epiphanios answers:

"As regards the saying [commemoration] of the names of the dead, what could be more useful, more proper and wonderful? For this causes those present to believe that the departed live and are not in a state of non-existence, but rather that they exist and live with the Master; and it causes that the holy kerygma be proclaimed, that there is [lit. there being] hope for those brethren who are prayed for, who are, as it were, in a distant land. And indeed the prayer made in their behalf brings profit, though in truth, it does not do away with all their offences, because in this world, we often do wrong involuntarily and voluntarily, and this act [of praying about the sins of the reposed] clearly points out that which is more perfect. For, we commemorate both just and sinners...."

St John Chrysostom, as we saw above, assures us of benefits from our prayers for those fallen asleep. What reason does he give for these prayers?

"And this is the reason for the prayers, psalms and glorifications of God [at burial services]: so that you not weep and lament, but rather give thanks to God Who has taken him."

As we saw above, according to our apostolic

father Saint Dionysios, the prayers and commemoration of the reposed serve primarily to educate the faithful regarding the promises given to those who struggle for salvation, He declares that the things we ask on behalf of the reposed are only proclamations of what they are going to receive, because God has already promised them, and so far from Him requiring our prayers in order that the reposed be shown mercy, He readily, without our prompting, overlooks those sins and stains of the faithful. He does not keep some kind of "scorecard" but knows the heart and the volition and the disposition of the soul, and this He "accounts to us for righteousness" on account of Christ.

Saint John of Kronstadt also captures the immensity and beauty of the true meaning of our commemorations of the reposed when, separating himself from the corrupted textbook theology, he turns to his own deep patristic consciousness and proclaims:

"What a close connection there is between the Church in heaven and the Church on earth! What love the Church has! Behold how She unceasingly remembers, calls upon in prayer and glorifies the Church in heaven for the great deeds accomplished on earth for God's sake; She unceasingly prays for the

Church on earth and intercedes for the departed, in the hope of their resurrection, of their life eternal and of their union with God and the saints. Her love is immense, great, divine! Let us enter into the spirit of this love of our Mother, the Orthodox Church, and let us be penetrated with the spirit of this love. Let us look upon all our brethren as our own members, upon ourselves and them as members of one body of the Church, and let us love them actively, as ourselves; then we ourselves shall be living members of the Church in heaven and she will be our active and speedy helper and intercessor.

"How do we maintain [this] connection with the spiritual world, with the heavenly Church? By calling upon them in prayer, by keeping the festivals instituted in their [those fallen asleep] honour; and by the Church services. For the Church is one, under one Head __ Christ. How do we maintain [this] connection with the departed? By means of prayers for them, especially when united with the offering of the bloodless sacrifice. How do we maintain union with living Christians...Again, by means of prayer for them all in God's temple and also at home."

Here is the true meaning of all our prayers and commemorations of the faithful fallen asleep, that we be mindful of them and of God's promise to the faithful, that we learn and assimilate a deep, unshakable understanding of the uniqueness and unity of the Holy Church, and of Her hope and joy, so that we too might grow in love and be given the courage to struggle to attain those promises for ourselves. We commemorate the reposed so that we remain consciously united with them, confessing our faith in the resurrection and life eternal.

Our prayers for the reposed are manifestations of Christian love, hope and faith, and they are revelations of the mystery of the union of heaven and earth in the body of the Holy Church. The immense difference between this pure, patristic understanding and the Scholastic concept is dramatically demonstrated if we compare these words of St John of Kronstadt, in which he obviously expresses his own deep spiritual conscience, with his words in another place, in which he expresses the textbook teaching on the subject of prayers for the reposed.

Compare the above-quoted words of St John of Kronstadt with the explanation of the daily liturgies offered for the reposed, given by the most venerable and authoritative commentator on the liturgical practices of the Church, St Symeon of Thessaloniki:

"...and especially [is] the Bloodless Sacrifice offered daily, for there is nothing more profitable for him who has fallen asleep, nor is there anything so much a cause of joy, illumination and union with God, for then, the very Blood of the Lord is shed in behalf of us the worthless ones, and the Divine Body is sacrificed ....What indeed is more beneficial than for Christ to be sacrificed in our behalf?

The particle [taken out of the prosphora] at the awesome sacrifice and the commemoration made then of him that has departed unites him to God and invisibly grants him to partake and to participate in Him. For this reason, not only the brethren who have in repentance departed in Christ are greatly benefited, comforted and saved, but also the sacred and divine souls of the saints greatly rejoice in this...and through this most sacred sacrifice, they more purely and lucidly are united to Christ and commune and more truly partake of His gifts."

Do we not see that not only sinful believers, such as we, benefit from these prayers, but also the saints? And we all benefit in the same manner, for these prayers are great mysteries of divine love. Great indeed is the power of Godly love, and great is the mystery of divine love in the Holy Church. For, such love ascends to heaven and penetrates even the darkness of Hades.

To those in Hades, it gives some small remission of the darkness – for love, which is the essence of all goodness, is the essence of spiritual light, before which darkness must retreat – and it gives, by God's grace, some kind of merciful and ineffable comfort and relief. But to those reposing in paradise, the prayers of the Holy Church rise up like warm waves of love which encompass the soul like a mother's tender embrace, like the gentle kiss a mother plants on the forehead of a sleeping child in the middle of the night. As God's grace is borne on the wings of His love, so our love is borne on the wings of God's grace, and by grace the souls of the departed perceive our love, and by His grace, they benefit from our prayers and alms offered in love on their behalf. For, all things which the soul perceives, it perceives not of itself, but by the action of divine grace, just as it remains immortal not of itself, but by grace.

The benefits which the reposed derive from these daily liturgies and commemorations are not in the form of forcing God to mercy or buying off demons but in the form of spiritual increase. The Church, as a loving mother, desires that all Her children have the best, or at least better. The reposed member of the Church is still a member: the organism of which he was and is a cell has not ceased to function to the fullest.

That functioning (which is certainly soteriological and pertains to the spiritual development of all Her members) involves the whole created universe, which is being redeemed along with man. It certainly involves the reposed in some way. The grave does not form a barrier to the love and life of the Holy Church (and that life is a liturgical life); the co-suffering love of the body of the faithful extends to all alike and penetrates the grave and "Hades."

The saints, though glorified already and interceding for us, derive benefit from our commemoration of them, and we pray for them and for all for the sake of their increase, so that, by God's hand, love is made manifest, and they pass from light to light, from joy to joy, from glory to glory, every good and every perfect thing being made more perfect, more radiant by the divine action of godly love, in the which all are bound together and ascend as one body toward the perfection of our high calling in Christ.

What is so marvellous that we ask for the "pardon and remissions of the sins" of our reposed brothers and sisters? Not as though God would not grant it anyway, and not as though they would not be saved even without our prayers, but as demonstrating our oneness and unity of love. And what is so marvellous that the fathers on occasion phrased their charge to us to pray for the departed as if our prayers were the effectual means of the remission of their sins? For God honours love and things done from love, and the gifts of love even from us poor sinners He in no wise rejects or turns away, but in His own perfect love, He causes that our gifts of prayers and alms be received by the souls of the reposed and that they benefit from them.

For He does not allow that godly love be offered in vain but as the Author of love, He causes His work to be fulfilled. In this sense we say that the reposed benefit from our prayers and receive, as it were, pardon and remission of the consequences of sins on account of our prayers.

Is this any different from what the sponsor does for a child at baptism? Only in the first instance, the child must accept, in due time, this intent, those vows made in its behalf and complete and fulfil what has been begun on its behalf, but the reposed believer has already accepted this intent before his death, by his very faith in the Holy Church which only helps complete and perfect what he has already begun. Would God deny grace and salvation to the child if there were no sponsor to proclaim the promises and vows? Of course not, and neither would He hinder the soul of the faithful even if no-one so much as breathed a prayer in their behalf. Nor would the demons have the slightest tyranny over the soul just because it had no-one to utter some magical incantations to force them to release it.

But what is it, then, to have their "sins pardoned and remitted" by the prayers of the faithful? Is it not that their own conscience is relieved of its burden by the light of our love generated in the serving of the Holy Mysteries for the person? For, they know already that they are "saved" and destined for the Kingdom, but perhaps their conscience is still troubled by the burden of its own self-knowledge. The conscience is, after all, our only accuser.

Nonetheless, this much is clear, that God allows the manifestation of our love and prayers to be received by the souls of the reposed, in order to increase their joy and give them the comfort of the feeling of oneness and companionship common to the Body of Christ, the Holy Church leading us in the struggle of love "till we all come in the unity of the faith, and of the knowledge of the Son of God, unto a perfect man, unto the measure of the stature of the fulness of Christ: that we be no more...tossed to and fro and carried about by every wind....But speaking the truth in love, may grow up into Him in all things, which is the Head, even Christ: from Whom the whole body fitly joined together and united by that which every joint supplies, according to the effectual working in the measure of every part, making increase of the body unto the edifying of itself in love" (Eph.4:13-16.)

For believers, death is not an object of fear or terror. No-one who has lived a life of active faith need tremble in terror at death. For, "death is a fair - haven" (St John Chrysostom), and "no-one should be made sad by death; since in living there is a labour and peril, in dying, peace and the certainty of resurrection" (St Cyprian of Carthage), moreover, "I believe the words of the wise that every fair and God-beloved soul, when it departs hence, immediately enjoys a sense and perception of the blessings which await it...and feels a wondrous pleasure and exultation, and goes rejoicing to meet its Lord" (St Gregory the Theologian), and "Whether we live, we live unto the Lord; whether we die, we die unto the Lord: whether we live therefore, or die, we are the Lord's" (Paul). Our holy and God bearing father Gregory the Theologian "trusts the word of the wise" that the soul departs the body and at once enjoys the noetic awareness of its future blessings, that the souls of the faithful go forth from the body "rejoicing to meet its Lord," feeling "a wondrous exultation." In the words of our apostolic father St. Dionysios:

"..the divine love overlooking, through its goodness, the stains which have come to them through human infirmity, since no one, as the Scripture says, is free of blemish."[2]

Compare the gruesome, complex and legalistic mythologies about demonic torture chambers, aerial traffic courts and wandering souls needing to be prayed to rest, with the pure, simple and profoundly Christian explanations of the apostles and fathers of the memorial services and prayers offered for the reposed on the third, ninth and fortieth days, and the yearly anniversary of their demise. The holy apostles have commanded us to, "Let the third day of the departed be celebrated with psalms and lessons and prayers, on account of Him Who arose on the third day; and let the ninth day be celebrated in remembrance of the living, and of the departed; and the fortieth day according to the ancient pattern: for so did the people lament Moses, and the anniversary day in memory of him. And let alms be given to the poor out of his goods for a memorial of him."[3]

Turning again to that foremost authority on Orthodox liturgical practices, St Symeon of Thessaloniki, we learn:

"[The Kolyva is offered] because man is also a seed and like a fruit from the earth; and like a seed sown in the earth he will be raised up again by God's might....The tritia [third day service] is celebrated for the reason that [the reposed one] received his being through the Trinity and having passed to a state of good being and being changed he shall [at the resurrection] appear in his original state or one superior. The ennata [ninth day] is celebrated that his soul dwell together with the holy the [nine orders of] angels, being immaterial and naturally similar to them – for these spirits are nine in number and by them [the orders] they triply proclaim and praise the God in Trinity – and so that he may be united with the holy spirits of the saints. The tessaracosta [fortieth] is celebrated because of the Saviour's ascension – which came to pass after so many days after His Resurrection – in the sense that he [the reposed] as it were, having also risen and having ascended, as it were, being caught away in the clouds, shall meet the Judge and being united with Him, he should ever be with the Lord (1Ths.4:17).

Now the third, sixth and ninth months also celebrated as proclaiming the Trinity, the God of all, and His glory in behalf of the deceased, for by the Trinity a man is fashioned, and when loosed from the body he returns to Him, and by the Trinity he hopes to receive resurrection. But the end of the year is celebrated because it is the consummation, and our God, the Trinity, is the Life of all and the Cause of being, and shall be the restoration of all and the renewal of human nature."[4]

St Gregory the Theologian explains his own offering of a memorial to Caesarios:

Such is my offering; if it be slight and inferior to his worth, God loves that which is according to our power. Part of our gift is complete, the remainder we will pay by offering (those of us who still survive) every year our honours and memorials."[5]

Thus, we have presented the specific, pure, simple, joyous doctrine of the holy apostles and fathers concerning things done for those who have fallen asleep.

Finally, beloved in Christ, let us recall those words of the Apostle cited earlier, that:

"Because of Him the whole body is joined and firmly held together by the joints and ligaments with which it is supplied, according to the effectual working in the measure of every part, grows to full maturity, building itself up in love," ."..holding the Head [Jesus Christ], from Whom all the body by joints and bands having nourishment ministered, and knit together, increases with the increase of God" (Eph.4:13-16;[6] Col.2:19).

And if we are all thus knit together, it is by the power of divine love, and our prayers and commemorations of those fallen asleep are but the confession and manifestation of the penetration of the

75

faithful by this divine love, a grace-filled response of love to love. This is not of ourselves, but it is the grace of God working in those who accept it, "both to will and to do of His own good pleasure" (Phil.2: 13).

THE MEMORIAL SERVICES OF THE THIRD, NINTH AND FORTIETH DAYS:
A patristic explanation of these services. A refutation of the false "Makarian Homily." An exposition of the heresies in the false "Makarian Homily." An explanation about the actual source of the "Makarian Homily."

The Fictitious "Makarian Document" Concerning The Memorial Services.

The following is a critique of a tale which has been attributed to St Makarios of Alexandria. It purports to give an explanation of the Christian tradition of offering memorial services for the departed on the third, ninth and fortieth days after their repose.

Ordinarily, one might consider this fable to be a mere "pious fraud," a pretty little tale with some ethical value, despite its obvious pagan overtones and, therefore, harmless. That is not the case with this fable, however, because it is not "harmless." Not only are the clearly Gnostic and pagan elements of it almost always taken at face value by simple readers and even educated clergy, thus introducing pagan ideas into the minds of the faithful, but the tale keeps people, even seminarians, from reading the *actual* patristic and apostolic explanations of the third, ninth and fortieth day commemorations for the departed.

The Makarian document contains serious heresies, long ago refuted by the holy fathers of the Orthodox Church. Moreover, because of this fictitious document, practically no-one ever reads the actual Orthodox Christian teaching on the subjects it deals with. To the contrary, cluttered, foggy, pagan and Gnostic mythology is being foisted off on Christians, in place of the clear, simple, scriptural truth of the Orthodox reasons for the third, ninth and fortieth day memorial services.

We have arranged this examination of the Makarian document in two columns. On the one side is the Makarian document itself and in the opposite column are relevant teachings of the holy and God-bearing fathers. In this way, a direct comparison may be made. At the end, we will discuss more at length the heretical aspects of the Makarian document. Essentially, the heresies are: (1) the idea that a soul can wander about after it has departed the body; (2) the idea of a radical dualism between soul and body; (3) the idea that souls are already in hell, suffering in the "fire." Another aspect of the fable almost too ridiculous to be considered a heresy is the idea that a person or the soul of a person could stand before the very throne of God, reverence Him in His Heavenly

Kingdom, and afterward be led into hell.

THE MAKARIAN FABLE

According to the fable, St Makarios of Egypt was walking along the road, chatting with some angels which were strolling along with him. No one knew the reason for the memorial services offered by the Church for those who had departed, so he decided to ask the angels about it. One of the angels who was strolling with him replied:

When, on the third day, the body is brought into the church, the soul of the dead person receives from his Guardian Angel some relief from the grief which he feels at parting from his body. He receives this relief because of the oblation and praise which are offered in his behalf in God's temple, from which a blessed hope arises in him. For, over the time of two days, the soul has to wander at random over the world, with the angels accompanying it. Since the soul loves its body, it sometimes hovers about in the house in which it was parted from the body; sometimes around the coffin in which its body has been placed. Thus it passes those days like a bird

THE ORTHODOX CHRISTIAN TEACHING

Condemnation of All Teachings That the Soul Can Wander After Death:

"Nor, indeed, is it possible for a soul, once separated from its body, to wander here anymore. For, `the souls of the righteous are in the hands of God.'... And the souls, also of sinners, are straightaway led away hence... And it cannot be that a soul, when it has gone out of the body can wander here" (St John Chrysostom, *Homily 28 on Matthew*.)

The Actual Orthodox Teaching About the Meaning of the Third, Ninth and Fortieth Day Services:

The holy apostles have commanded us to, "Let the third day of the departed be celebrated with psalms and lessons and prayers, on account

79

which seeks a nesting place for itself. The good soul, however, wanders through those places where it used to perform good deeds of righteousness.

On the third day, *every* soul is brought to heaven, that it may do reverence to the God of all. Wherefore, the Church has the blessed custom of offering oblation and prayers on the third day for that soul.

After the soul has done reverence to God, He commands that it be shown the varied and fair mansions of the saints and the beauty of paradise. All these things the soul sees during six days, marvelling and giving glory to God, the Creator of all. When the soul has seen all these things, it is changed and forgets all the sorrows which it felt in the body.. ..

Having thus viewed the joys of the righteous for the space of six days, the angels lead the soul again to do reverence to God. Therefore, the Church does well to celebrate and offer oblation for the soul on the ninth day.

After this second reverencing of God, the Master of all orders that the soul be conduc- of Him Who arose within the space of three days; and let the ninth day be celebrated in remembrance of the living, and of the departed; and the fortieth day according to the ancient pattern: for so did the people lament Moses, and the anniversary day in memory of him. And let alms be given to the poor out of his goods for a memorial of him." *The Instructions of the Holy Twelve Apostles, Bk.8, Ch.42.*

Turning again to that foremost authority on Orthodox liturgical practices, St Symeon of Thessaloniki, we learn:

"[The Kolyva is offered] because man is also a seed and like a fruit from the earth; and like a seed sown in the earth he will be raised up again by God's might....The tritia [third day service] is celebrated for the reason that [the reposed one] received his being through the Trinity and having passed to a state of good being and being changed he shall [at the resurrection] appear in his original state or one superior. The ennata [ninth day] is celebrated because his spirit [soul] abides together with the holy spirits, the angels, *being immaterial* ted to Hell, to be shown the places of torment, the different departments of Hell, the various torments of the impious, which causes the souls that are there to groan continually and gnash their teeth. Through these various places of torments, the soul is conducted for thirty days, trembling, lest it be also imprisoned therein.

On the fortieth day, the soul is again taken to do reverence to God; and only then does the Judge determine the fitting place for its imprisonment according to its deeds.

Thus, the Church acts properly in making mention of the baptized dead on the fortieth day.

[Since we are dealing in popular mythologies, one must wonder where the passage through the twenty-one aerial toll-houses fits into this schedule. The angels chatting with St Makarios evidently did not know about them, since the "passage through the toll-houses" supposedly occupies this entire forty day period.]

and naturally similar to them — for these spirits are [of] nine [orders] in number and by them [the orders] they triply proclaim and praise the God in Trinity — and so that he may be united with the holy spirits of the saints. The tessaracosta [fortieth] is celebrated because of the Saviour's ascension — which came to pass so many days after His Resurrection. *(On Things Done for the Departed.)*

Condemnation of the Heresy That There Are Souls Already in Hell and Suffering:

Nothing could more clearly expose the heresy and falseness of this fictitious "Makarian Homily" than the words of our Holy and God-bearing father, Mark of Ephesus, in his *Ten Arguments against Purgatory:*

"But if, as was said, no-one has entered either the Kingdom or Hell [Gehenna], how is it that we hear concerning the rich man and Lazarus that the former was in fire and torment and spoke with Abraham? The Lord said everything about Lazarus in the manner of a parable, even as He spoke of the ten virgins and in the rest of the parables. The parable of Lazarus has not come to pass in actuality, because the sinners in Gehenna shall not see the righteous who are with Abraham in the Kingdom, nor will any of them know his neighbour, being in that darkness.

"Accepting this opinion our Church thus is minded and preaches, and She is most ready and well prepared to defend it. Firstly, the Lord in the Gospel according to Matthew describes beforehand the judgment to come, saying, `Come, ye blessed of My Father, inherit..' — it is evident that they have not yet inherited — `the kingdom prepared for you;' `prepared' He says, not `already given.' But to sinners He says, `Depart ye cursed' — evidently they have not yet departed — into everlasting fire `prepared' not for you but `for the devil and his angels.' Here again He says `prepared,' since [that fire] has not yet received the condemned demons."

THE ORIGIN OF
THE "MAKARIAN HOMILY"

*The following is a reply to a letter which was received by the editor of **Orthodox Canada**. The reply to this letter included the preceding critique of the "Makarian Homily."*

As we have seen, the false Makarian "homily" does indeed differ radically from the actual Orthodox teachings, which few people seem interested to learn.

As to where it originated one can only surmise. However, one would probably be accurate to surmise that because they had always taken the practice for granted, and never sought to understand why it was done, some lingering ideas taken from the embalming texts[7] of pharaonic Egypt crept in. To "remedy" this, someone simply created an answer. This is certainly not unusual; this has happened many times in the past, and the fictitious explanation has frequently been given the name of a famous person as its supposed author. In the case of the memorial services, the answer was taken from pagan folklore. It was not at all unusual for someone to invent an "answer" like this and attribute it to someone with more authority, and this was a notable and regular practice of the early Gnostic sects. That is why there were so many false "Gnostic Gospels" and fake "apostolic epistles" around before the Ecumenical Councils sorted them out and determined which ones were false. The story about the wandering soul probably actually did come from Egypt, because the tale comes directly from Egyptian paganism, from the rites of embalming high ranking personages of the old Egyptian kingdom.

The embalming process took from forty to seventy days (it took longer in the most ancient era, and closer to forty days in later times, longer for the wealthy and noble, a shorter time for ordinary people). In early Egypt, the period of mourning, which was taken quite seriously, could last for a year or more. Sometime in later Egypt, the official mourning time had been set at forty days. The stages of this mourning process were marked off with special significance for each, relating to the steps of the embalming ritual. In fact, we read in the Bible that Joseph, who was given a high rank in Egypt, and thus had access to the embalming rite of the nobility, had his father embalmed.

"And Joseph commanded his servants, the physicians, to embalm his father, and the physicians embalmed Israel [Jakob]. And **forty days were fulfilled for him; for so are fulfilled the days of those who are embalmed"** *[in Egypt] (Gn. 50:2-3).*

We can read about this practice in the history of Herodotos, the "father of history." He records the same information about the embalming process during his visit to Egypt (c.440 B.C.).

In Egyptian mythology, the soul itself could not rest until the body had been properly prepared for burial, thus, the pagans believed that the soul wandered for this time. It is a fact that the embalmed body was often kept in its family home for some time after the rites. There was a belief that the soul haunted the house for some period during this time, and needed to be able to find its body. During that period, according to Egyptian paganism, the soul was judged and weighed before the forty two nome gods (a source, by the way, of the equally pagan "aerial tollhouse" myth, which reduces the nome gods to exactly half: twenty one in number, but the "sins" decided at each follows the pagan Egyptian pattern very closely).

It is a fact that official or taboo periods for celebrating, commemorating or fearing the reposed are not at all of Christian origin, rather certain logical periods already used in pre-Christian practice were chosen and "baptised" into Christian practice. For example, in voodoo practice, the ninth day is especially significant, as it has been in pagan practice from very ancient times. If a person has been murdered, their body is often buried with a whip or weapon in each hand so that, on the ninth day, the dead person can revenge itself on the murderer. A solemn, often dark celebration may be kept on that day by voodoo practitioners. We note in the Scripture that the forty days kept for Joseph were not kept because of any Jewish practice or ordinance of God, but because "it was the custom of the Egyptians." The purely symbolic meanings given to these practices by the apostles and early fathers was intended to give a Christian understanding and

RESPONSE OF THE LATE V.REV. FR. MICHAEL POMOZANSKY TO A LETTER OF FR. PUHALO CONCERNING PRAYERS FOR THE DEAD.

(This letter was translated from Russian to English at Holy Trinity Monastery, Jordanville, N.Y. and forwarded to Fr Puhalo by Archbishop Laurus).

The Apostle Paul teaching his disciple the apostle Timothy, "how one ought to conduct himself in the house of God, which is the Church of the Living God" (1 Tm.3:15), writes to him in the second epistle: "But in a great house there are not only vessels of gold and silver, but also of wood and of earth; and some to honour, and some to dishonour [or, base usage]" (2 Tm.2:20). The Apostle has in mind the people in the Church when he speaks of vessels, but we have the right of employing his thought in a simpler and more literal, yet still a broader sense.

The history of the Orthodox Christian Church, continuing from the Apostles, has now come to the end of its second millennium of existence. Throughout the process of her broad and many sided growth, the Church has diligently preserved only the truths of the faith, the dogma of faith. Upon their foundation the tree of the Church developed in all directions, nourished by the Grace of the Spirit of God. The wealth of its spiritual contents on its own increased, and at the same time its material contents grew, and often the one would give place to the other. Much was acquired simply for preservation; other things have been carried away by the river of time into the realm of the forgotten, and now on certain rare occasions, something may float to the surface, thanks to the efforts and searches of special investigators and researchers. The Church herself regards everything conservatively and patiently (indulgently), and it has no persons who are assigned to the task of separating the valuable from that which is not so valuable. It has been forced only at certain times to uproot tares from the field of wheat, both in the spiritual and in the material sense. From such a conservative attitude, the Church does not suffer any harm. It happens sometimes that something which seems of little value later turns out to be both beneficial and important. The Church, as it were, says, those losses suffered as a result of the persecutions of the Church and of Christianity, wars and the destruction of elements of nature are sufficient. If we are to speak of literature (written works), the Church rejects only that which is an evilly intended forgery or a heretical concoction.

Let us speak a bit concerning genuine Church literature. All the various forms of literature are not of the same value; among them there is a graduation of value passing from sanctity all the way to simple usefulness.

Here, approximately, are these graduations:

1. The four Gospels which are kept in the Sanctuary on the Holy Table.
2. The Epistles and Paromea (Old Testament Prophecies).
3. The Liturgicons and main divine service books.

The above are the legacy of the temple.

4. Patristic literature.
5. Lives of saints.

These latter, while they may be read in Church, are primarily for private reading.

6. Theological science, academic theology and various theological literature.

7. Ecclesiastical and historical sciences, practical textbooks and reference manuals.

8. Pious accounts, edifying parables. These are simply morally inspiring readings in an easy form that is accessible to all.

We ask to be excused for such a lengthy introduction. Let us now pass on to the question concerning prayer for the dead in the article in question [i.e., an article in *Orthodox Life* which prompted our letter and the writing of this present book].

One must agree with the author of the letter [Fr Puhalo]. The article has essential weaknesses.

We are talking about the Church's commemoration of the dead. Part of the material in the article is concerned with the teaching of the Church, dogmatic theology; but another part with pious accounts and, finally, with Church and popular customs. In the [Orthodox Life] article there is no distinction made concerning the dignity of the material presented and thus matters which do not concern the dogma of the Church are dogmatized. Let us point out what we have in view:

We find an appropriate example of this in the footnotes of the author. There is no need to discuss the prayerful or liturgical meaning of "kolyva", as an offering for the dead. For it is simply an expressing of the desire to treat those who participated in the prayers for the dead, thank them for their love, as the Apostle says: "all is good and there is nothing worthy of condemnation that is done with the word of God in prayer." Even more so, there is no use in explaining the "meaning" of the wheat in the kolyva or what the honey and sugar in it "mean" or "symbolize".

In accordance with ancient views, it is accepted to offer special prayers on the third and fortieth days; these days, these very numbers in the Scripture, in general, represent something sacred. But the Church does not teach that commemoration on these days, as on the ninth day, is "indispensable". "Man was not made for the Sabbath but the Sabbath for man." The days are not the important point.

In such points of the article as the quantity of commemorations, of their ritual forms (candles, prosphora), the skeptical reader could even read in the material interests of the clergy or the parish church; people are given to such criticism.

"The Church established" we read [in the Orthodox Life article], but in fact only one thing is necessary and required for the believer. Other things are offered and regulated by the Church for good order and benefit. A third category is permitted as a good intention or custom which has arisen among the people of the Church and these are given their proper forms for the Church.

In connection with this, there arises a question which the author of the letter does not himself pose, but which is essential.

Do the dead *need* prayers from us? Can the sins of a man be removed by the prayers of other men? The answer is simple. We know that the Church is, in all its depth, a "bond of love", where there is One for all — Christ. Therefore in His Body, the Church, one must pray for all and all for each. This idea is expressed in our services, especially in the prayers of the priest. We pray for those close to us as a duty of love regardless of whether our brother or sister needs our prayers or even wants them.

Much regarding prayers for the dead can appear illogical. We note that the more devout a person was, the more prayers are offered for his repose. The Church is, as it were, indifferent to great sinners and apostates. Why is this? And in general, do the dead need our prayers? God Himself is merciful and loves mankind, and would He not forgive the dead person without our praying for him? The answer is given in the Gospel and the Epistles of the Apostles. In them there are given three axioms of Christianity: death does not exist; pray for one another; love never fails (Rm.14; Js.5; 1 Cor.13).

Let us now go on to the material in the article [in

Orthodox Life] which specifically called forth the concern of the author of the letter [Fr Puhalo]. We think it possible that this concern expresses also the concern of others. We allow the thought that our Eastern, traditional Church in the sphere of religious psychology is not so strict in the demand for being logical as the Western, which is brought up in a more rationalistic direction; however, allow us to state our understanding of the matter.

We mentioned at the beginning "pious accounts" which are in the article. Our Eastern, pious readers from ancient times have loved to read anthologies of brief, easy stories from the lives of the ascetics, the desert fathers, concerning their journeys, their struggles, their meetings with one another, their conversations, their relation to the desert around them, and to the humble and at the same time miraculous revelations in their lives and acts. Up to the most recent times, such anthologies have been popular, such as "The Spiritual Meadow," and the "Lausiac History". These little stories often contain in their naive simplicity much that is allegorical and moral instruction. They are not historical material, and therefore it is not so important as to who is named in the account or whom specifically it concerns.

For example, the account of the conversation of St Makarios with the skull he found. This conversation attracts attention because of its originality. The skull says that it was formerly that of a pagan priest. But what is its meaning? In the way of life of the person whose brain once worked in the skull? Hardly. "Makarios listened and placed the skull on the earth and buried it." Did Makarios not think to pray for the man? To make the sign of the cross over him? Or to sympathize with him? Why? Because this is hopeless. And this would even have been sinful. But he does not throw his discovery on the ground, but buries it; in this way he expresses his respect for the man. And this is edifying. But what about the conversation? It is an allegory, a parable. But it also might be the spiritual insight of a holy person. Do the Holy Scriptures not offer us examples of such spiritual insight?

A separate question, and perhaps even a protest was evoked from the author of the letter [Fr Puhalo] by the account of the dream of Theodora concerning the toll houses, in the life of Basil the New. What is this dream needed for, when it introduces into the heavenly sphere concepts and actions which are purely earthly — the image of toll houses or customs stations in heaven, images or arguments for the soul between angels and demons? Let us reply that all this is expressed in a dream, the dream of the disciple of Basil the New, and it is given as an account of what the disciple saw in this dream. Our dreams are also in the form of tangible and earthly images. And at the same time our dreams can be allegorical. *They can express our emotional state, our imagination, and often our illness both of body and soul, dressing them in the form of living beings.*

In this instance the dream is recounted just as it was. We might allow that the narrator of the life of Basil the New put it into a certain order, put the sins of people into a certain scheme, as this is generally accepted among ascetic writers. But regardless, it is thanks to this full scheme of the falls and weaknesses of men that the account attracted such attention and became so popular among persons seeking moral perfection. *But of course this dream is allegorical and is made up of a series of symbols.* We are earthly, and we cannot speak of heavenly things with any other language than our earthly tongue; we do not know the tongues of angels. In the Psalms we address the Ruler of All: "Incline Thine ear; stretch forth Thy right hand; draw out Thy sword; chastise and defend with Thy high arm."

The Metropolitan of Moscow, Makary, reminds us that we should understand such accounts in as lofty (spiritual) a manner as possible. We can only accept his advice.

Let us take this earthly side of the symbolism into the spiritual understanding. Theodora is the soul of man; the angels — its virtues; the demons — its sins.

Both are in the soul of a man and perhaps after death are found, as it were, on the scales of a balance. Is this image inconsistent with our religious concepts? Talking about the "balance" we imitate the symbolism contained in our hymns: "Thy Cross is found as the measure between two thieves; for the one was brought down to Hades by the weight of blasphemy, but the other was lightened of his sins unto the knowledge of theology: O Christ God, glory to Thee" (Troparion of the 9th Hour).

ENDNOTE:

1. P.G.96:33A.

2. *The Ecclesiastical Hierarchy,* Ch.7. (Complete text in Appendix 1, *the Soul, the Body and Death* (Synaxis Press, 1991).

3. *The Instructions of the Holy Twelve Apostles,* Bk.8, Ch.42.

4. *On Things Done for the Departed.*

5. *Panegyric for Caesarios.*

6. This is a more exact translation than the KJV.

7. "The Egyptian Book of the Dead." The ancient Egyptians believed that the soul wandered near the body and in familiar places until the vital organs had been removed and placed in canopic jars. The soul could not continue its journey until the brain had been. Then it continued to pass through the judgment of the Nome gods (toll stations).

APPENDIX 1
DISCUSSION ON MARRIAGE
(Extracts From Discussions about Marriage
From Vladika Lazar's Conversations about Marriage)

LOVE WITHOUT COMMITMENT IS A LIE

Though I speak with the tongues of men and of angels, and do not have love, I am as the sound of brass and a noisy cymbal...Love is longsuffering and kind; love does not envy; love does not boast of itself nor is it puffed up. Love does not behave itself in an unseemly manner, nor seek to have its own way; it is not easily provoked and does not think evil. Love does not rejoice in iniquity, but in truth; it bears all things, believes all things, endures all things. Love never fails... When I was a child, I spoke as a child, I understood as a child, I thought as a child: but when I became an adult, I put away childish things ...Now, there abides faith, hope and love: but the greatest of these is love (1Cor. 13).

Of all the faculties, senses, capabilities, attributes and virtues of the human race, it is committed love that bestows upon us our humanity and re- lates us to the Divine. Love is the dynam- ic force, which gives meaning to our lives in this world and our hope for eternity. While the nature of genuine love may seem elusive and indefinable, it is a force that takes us outside ourselves and unites and bonds us to a greater reality in a positive and creative manner. It is a tragedy that the word "love" is so often used as a metaphor for "gratification," "self-fulfilment," or for using another person to fulfil our sexual passions.

Love gives meaning and purpose to life by spiritually bonding us together with another person (as in marriage), with other people (as in a parish or other extended family), and with God, in a way that gives depth, meaning, permanence, commitment and a positive, creative dimension, to all that we share in life and, indeed, to life itself. Love, for an Orthodox Christian, is, above all the dynamic force of salvation, of ascension toward God. Marriage is, first and foremost, a path to salvation.

There is no such thing as love without a firm commitment. Not realizing the full meaning and implications of love is one of the main reasons young people engage in pre-marital sexual relations, and also the single most important reason that so many marriages fail.

The commitment of love is expressed in the sincere desire, arising from the depths of heart and soul, to forsake every consideration of self and subject every other attachment for the sake of the one we love. In true love, ambition for self-glory and advancement is transformed into a desire to please and care for the one we love. Individual interests are replaced by mutual interests, and "my" life is dissolved into "our" life. We commit our- selves to a spiritual bond which is a type and likeness of Christ and the Church, a likeness of self-sacrifice that brings with it the joy of hope and expectation and salvation and everlasting life.

Marriage is a type and likeness of redemption itself.Many times, people think that they "fall in love," but this is almost never true. A couple may like each other very much— even intensely — and feel a strong sexual attraction, and these powerful feelings are interpreted as a strong love. Unfortunately for the girl or woman in such a situation, if they fall into pre-marital sexual relations, they will find that the man's "love" was often no more than his drive for conquest and that there was no basis for a genuine commitment.

It is, therefore, important that children and young people always be taught the absolute bond between love and complete commitment. Love is a "growth situation." No one actually "falls in love." People may like each other deeply and be strongly attached to each other, but love comes only from long-term experience. Commitment to one another is the prime expression of love and it gives strength to a relationship so that it can have time to grow and develop into a full and complete love. Without a fulfilled commitment, sexual relations are merely using another person for the most selfish of reasons.

Love pertains not only to the things we find positive and attractive in a person but also to the negative aspects of their personality and the things we discover about them over the years that we find unattractive. This is why actual love is not instantaneous. It is a process of growth and maturity.

None of us are "complete packages." We are all constantly changing, hopefully growing and developing. No two people grow and develop at the same rate and to the same degree. Unfortunately, some of us stop growing mentally, emotionally and spiritually and begin to stagnate and then degenerate. Often, the elusive, almost undefinable gradual breakdown in a marriage is precisely this difference in the growth and development of the partners. It does not matter whether both partners are working outside the home or the wife is working in the home, one of the two will almost certainly mature more quickly and more completely, and the spiritual, emotional and intellectual growth rate may very easily be different. This difference in development can cause a subtle arising of a gulf or division between a couple, and often neither party realizes the source of the gradual feeling of "drifting apart." If they do realise it, it can be difficult to discuss in a positive manner.

Men often feel threatened by a wife's growth, and women who work in the home often feel oppressed and "cheated" of the opportunity to grow.In a relationship with true love and commitment, a couple should grow and develop not merely with each other but because of each other. It is important to realize the possibility of this problem arising and discuss it at the beginning of a marriage. Indeed, it should be an integral part of the pre-marital counselling. Personal and individual growth, maturing and development should be planned for and, from the very beginning of an Orthodox marriage, it should be resolved that this process will be founded on genuine spiritual growth. It should be clearly understood that mutual spiritual growth and development is a fundamental reason for an Orthodox marriage in the first place. If this is clearly established, and the possibility of differing rates of intellectual and emotional maturing is understood from the beginning, it will be infinitely easier to cope with such a problem if it should arise. Any family, whether it consists only of husband and wife or includes a number of children, must constantly struggle to grow, develop and mature spiritually, emotionally and intellectually together, as a unit. This is difficult to accomplish and, from an Orthodox perspective, it requires much prayer and a clearly Christ-centred family life.

It is evident that this growth and development is something that must be carefully planned for in pre-marriage discussions and during the early years of marriage. From an Orthodox Christian perspective, it is an essential part of the reason for a couple to want to marry each other and it is a fundamental aspect of the very nature of marriage.

If there is a firm commitment to each other between two people, then there can be mutual growth and development in love, no matter what other divergent directions the two people's development may take. Their common ground for growth and development, indeed, the pivot point of their lives, should be their spiritual advancement. With this shared in common, their commitment will be firm and certain and their growth in love will be permanent and continuous. If the common ground of Orthodox Christian spiritual growth and development is established and accepted as the basis of a couple's life, then divergent paths of growth in other areas will not create difficulties in a marriage. The commitment of love requires that we keep our priorities clear.

Man was not created to exist in egoistic isolation, and man and woman are not two totally separate beings, for neither, can, on their own, fulfil God's command to be fruitful and multiply. Rather, they are two halves of one whole, called upon to dwell together in a sanctified unity, drawing together in an increasing love so that in such a state of oneness, they may rise from carnal to spiritual love and so aspire toward the Creator, having discovered through their own ascent in love, the hint of that higher and more perfect love that seeks freedom from the bonds of fleshly passions.

Marriage provides us with an opportunity and a means to grow and develop in the spiritual and emotional realm, but this growth and development can only take place on a firm foundation of genuine commitment to each other and a mutual, sincere commitment to God. The bond of unity and ever-growing love between husband and wife is designed to give humanity a basic experience and awareness of growth in love toward unity with God, made possible by Jesus Christ. Marriage, according to the Apostle, is a type of Christ and the Church (Eph.5: 32). It is intended to instruct us, not by means of abstract concepts or in books or words, but in an actual living experience, about Christ and the Church, and our whole relationship with God.

Love is intended to be first and foremost, a path of salvation, a path of ascension toward God. The commitment of love is an important aspect of this, for it defeats our ego and self-love, which are hindrances to our salvation and our relationship with God.

Marriage is not a legal or magical ritual for "making sexual relations moral." It is perfectly possible for sexual relations within a marriage to be immoral. If one party has entered into the marriage under false pretences and is living in it without genuine love, then, for that person, the relationship is not moral but merely a matter of utility or self-gratification. Love itself is the factor that makes the union moral. It is wrong to consider that the crowning ceremony is a magical means of changing something immoral into something moral. For, though marriage is sanctified by the Church, it is the condition and transformation of the heart which perfects and transfigures and saves.

All these things should be discussed in detail and prayerfully, not only with a couple who have decided to be married, but with teenagers, and in a more simple form, this should be gently woven into the children's church-school classes. The depth of commitment in marriage must be stressed, and the priest should make it clear that the commitment in marriage is not only between husband and wife, it is a commitment to God which involves the salvation of the soul. Marriage is, above all, a union of two people for the sake of mutually working out the salvation of their souls. Marriage is a means of ascent toward the heavenly kingdom.

THE MEANING OF MARRIAGE

Shall I tell you how marriage is also a mystery of the Church? Christ came into the Church, and She was made of Him and He united with Her in spiritual intercourse...So marriage is a type of the presence of Christ" (St John Chrysostom, Homily on Ephesians).

In the beginning, God created man and woman and called on them to unite as one, to live in unity and harmony, putting every other relationship aside. They were to be so spiritually united that they would be "as one flesh" (Gn.2: 24).

In paradise, this unity was real. After the fall, however, divisions occurred in our human nature, and the bond between husband and wife became corrupted. Because of this corruption, divorce was permitted (Nm.30:10-14) be- cause mankind's heart had become hardened (Mt.19:7-8). There was a certain amount of protection for a woman-particularly in relation to her dowry. However, apart from some social restrictions, divorce was simply a matter of the man telling the woman that the marriage was over. Marriage had lost its divine purpose and become only an agreement to live together, to "co-habit." Technically, it was reduced to a social and sexual function.

With the coming of Christ, something dramatic took place which changed the way marriage is understood.

Christ not only restored the original meaning of marriage but gave it the fulness of its meaning. Christ not only restored, in Himself, the original condition of man but in His humanity the destiny which Adam failed to attain his completed. As the "new Adam," He restores all things to their original intent and purpose. God's plan for mankind is reborn in Christ. The blessed condition of humanity in paradise was lost.[8]

Christ has reopened the gates of paradise and, in the Holy Church, planted anew the garden of Grace. The Kingdom of God has now been manifested on earth, and henceforth everything that takes place in the Christian life must be viewed in the context of the Heavenly Kingdom. Perhaps mankind has not yet returned to Eden, but paradise, in a spiritual form, has returned to mankind, and all who believe and accept the Kingdom must strive to draw away from the standards and concepts of the fallen world and come into accord with the standards and concepts of the Kingdom of God.

Spiritually, with the help of Christ and the Holy Spirit, man must rebuild paradise in his heart, or rather struggle to allow the Holy Spirit to manifest it there. The Kingdom must live within us now if we hope to abide in it for eternity.

Thus, for the Orthodox Christian, every step, every aspect of life is a Holy Mystery, a mystery of the Kingdom, and thus a part of the Mystery of Redemption. In the manifestation of the Heavenly Kingdom by Jesus Christ, marriage returns to its original intent, to the purpose for which it was created in paradise. It is once more a revelation of redemption, a type and likeness of Christ and the Church.

The being of mankind reveals the Church and its relationship to Christ our God, obscured though that revelation may have become. The human race, working together with Satan, has enslaved itself with senseless passions and negative stereotypes. Western man has excelled in this to such a degree that the true basis and purpose of human sex as a revelation has become completely obscured.

By sexuality, we do not mean "making love" (sex as a verb). "Sex"[9] is the whole fabric of an individual's being as either male or female. When human sex (gender, sic) and sexuality become imprisoned in stereotypes and moralistic bonds, then it is held back from rising to its true purpose.

That purpose itself is obscured in blind negatives. Human sexuality is at once deep and powerful, and yet as fine and delicate and beautiful as a fragile spring blossom. It is fascinatingly simple and pure while at the same time, one of the most complex, baffling and vulnerable aspects of our inter-human relations. These contradictory qualities are the conflict between the passions of the fallen nature and the purpose of the creation of human sexuality.

Man was created for communion with God. He can find his complete fulfilment only in a life of communion, praise and giving glory to the Creator, living in a unison of love with God, by love drawing nearer to Him, toward sharing in His immortality, in His Deity. We know that man was not created for death, that it was not God's intention for him to die, but rather to live through unity with the Creator. Yet God, Who knows all things from eternity unto eternity, foreknew humanity's fall from this state of unity and, thus, the advent of death. Because of this, He created Eve and provided every creature and living thing with a means of procreation. Man and woman were created so that even in the fallen state, they would have a means of a certain fulfilment in a type and revelation about Christ and the Church. The Apostle Paul, speaking to the Ephesians about the Mystery of marriage (which is also, in fact, the mystery of human sexuality), says: "This mystery is great, for I speak of Christ and the Church," and St John Chrysostom says:

> "Shall I tell you how marriage is also a mystery of the Church? Christ came into the Church, She was made of Him, and He

united with Her in spiritual intercourse...So marriage is a type of the presence of Christ."

Humans were not created to exist in egoistic isolation but to dwell together in a sanctified unity, drawing together in an increasing love so that in such a state of oneness, they may rise in spiritual love and so aspire toward the Creator, having discovered through their own ascent in love the hint of that higher and more perfect love which seeks freedom from the bonds of fleshly passions. The bond of unity and growing love between husband and wife is designed to give man the first basic experience and awareness of his growth in love toward unity with God, made possible by Christ Jesus.

Human sexuality is intended to reflect and thus to instruct us, not in totally abstract concepts or in books or words, but in actual living experience, concerning Christ and the Church and our whole relationship with God. In this revelation, the husband typifies Christ and the wife typifies the Church.

A MYSTERY OF GRACE

Marriage is a very great mystery of divine Grace. As a type of Christ and the Holy Church, Orthodox matrimony is also a profound revelation about the nature of our redemption. It reveals the fallen nature and teaches what Christ has done to redeem human nature through His Holy Church. Since the mystery of redemption has nothing to do with fulfilling or satisfying justice or purging some imaginary "Original Sin" but rather with the rescue and healing of human nature, enslaved by sin and the bondage of death, marriage is an ideal reflection of our redemption.

Christ came to earth to redeem human nature from the bondage of the Evil One and to regenerate us through the mystery of co-suffering love, a love so great,
so completely unselfish that the Immortal One Himself laid down His life for our sake. As Apostle Paul says: "Christ loved the Church and gave His life for Her" (Eph.5:25).

The creation of man and woman as opposites, as two separate parts of one whole, was a provision God made, fore-knowing man's fall. As such, it is a revelation about the separateness or division in the fallen human nature caused by sin, as St Basil the Great says:

"For there would be no divisions, no strife, no war among men, if sin had not made cleavages in human nature....And this is foremost in the Saviour's incarnate ekonomy: to gather human nature to itself and to Himself and, having abolished this evil cleavage, to restore the original unity, as the best physician binds up a body that has been broken in many pieces...."

Thus, marriage is a sanctified union of two people with different aspects of the human nature. This union joins the struggle of two individuals into a stronger, mutual effort for salvation. By growing in co-suffering, unselfish love for each other and their family, they conquer the fragmentation of human nature into isolated and self-centred individualism. This is stated clearly in the Prayer of Betrothal:

"O Lord, eternal God, Who has brought into unity and oneness the things which before, had been separate, Who blessed Isaak and Rebecca declaring them to be inheritors of Thy promise, bless these Thy servants...."

These same ideas are evident in the prayers throughout the service of the Holy Mystery of Matrimony, particularly in the most notable part of the service, the crowning. Traditionally, the bride and groom are crowned three times with "stefana," wreaths of laurel and blossoms, which, from ancient times, have symbolised victory, including the victory of the holy martyrs. At the time of the crowning ceremony, the husband and wife are led in a "cross procession" around the Gospel book three times. As they process, three hymns are chanted, which explain both the three-fold crowning and the profound meaning of marriage:

> "Rejoice, O Isaiah! For a virgin was truly with child and bore a Son, Emmanuel, Who is both God and Man: Dayspring is His name, and magnifying Him, we call the Virgin blessed."

The bride and groom are crowned with a crown of rejoicing. For Christ, as the Prophet foretold, has come into the world to reunite and redeem human nature, uniting it to Himself and regenerating it in His Holy Church. They are crowned with joy as types of Christ and His Holy Church, typifying that redemption, as they are united into one flesh by the Holy Spirit.

For the second crowning, as the couple processes around the Gospel, the people chant:

> "O holy martyrs who have fought the good fight and have received your crowns: entreat the Lord to have mercy on our souls."

The couple is also crowned with the martyr's crown. As Christ loved His Church and died for Her (Eph.5: 25), so also now the husband and wife are called upon to sacrifice their ego and self-love, to cease being "I" and become "we." They will sacrifice themselves for each other and, later, for their children, willingly "martyring" themselves, overcoming their ego and will for the sake of one another, out of love for each other. By this very act, they experience and grow in co-suffering love in imitation of Christ. In this, the human nature is healed and redeemed, if they will "run with patience the race which is set before them" (Hb. 12:1).

The third crowning, and circuit of the Gospel, is signified by the hymn:

> "Glory to Thee, O Christ God, Boast of the apostles and Joy of martyrs who proclaimed the Consubstantial Trinity."

The victory crown of salvation is bestowed upon the couple, for marriage is a union of two people into one flesh so that they can mutually work out their salvation by means of love, hope, joy, self-sacrificing and spiritual struggle. They have become both martyrs and apostles of Christ, striving to live His Gospel and teach it to their children, shepherding their families as the apostles and bishops shepherd the Church. Moreover, bride and groom have become something of a type of oneness of love of the Holy

Trinity, since "the two shall be one flesh" (Gn.2: 24; Mt.19:5),

"so that they are no longer two, but one flesh" (Mt.19: 6).

The original form of the Orthodox Christian marriage service was simple. The couple attended the Divine Liturgy and received Holy Communion together. The bishop then blessed them with a short prayer, asking God to unite the couple. The actual moment of the completion of the marriage was the joint reception of Holy Communion. This is straightforward and logical since marriage is a type and likeness of Christ and the Church. The Liturgy is the divine wedding feast of Christ and the Church, and Holy Communion is that moment in which the faithful— the Church — are supremely united to Christ. Holy Communion is a central point in our redemption. Marriage, as a direct type of the unity of Christ and the Church, is thus an event in the realm of redemption.

For Orthodox Christians, marriage is not simply a mutual agreement to live together in love and raise children in a legally sanctioned bond. It is a form of ministry, sealed by the Holy Spirit, in which the couple becomes living types of Christ and the Church, fulfilling the ministry of salvation toward each other, their children, and the whole Orthodox community.

MARRIAGE AND COVENANT

Brothers and sisters, marriage is not an accord between two people: it is a covenant between three: husband, wife, and God. Whoever is married in the Church has a covenant with God, Who created them male and female in the beginning, and ordained marriage as a revelation and prophecy, as a type of redemption and a revelation of His covenant with mankind.

When a couple has had their marriage crowned by the Church, their union is one specially sanctified "both on earth and in heaven" (Mt.16:19), and their marriage is not theirs alone, but is a matter of the whole "household of God," the whole body of Christ. This is why there is no justification for a "private marriage," which excludes any of the faithful from attendance. Marriage is a liturgical service in the presence of the "people of God." For the Orthodox Christian, the faithful—the people of God— are his or her immediate family, for they have a common father, God, and a common mother, the Church. A private, "by invitation only" wedding is not Orthodox and is contrary to the very essence of Orthodox marriage. Unless there is a compelling reason, a priest has no reason to serve such a marriage because every Liturgical service is an affair of the household of God, of the assembly of the "people of God."The

Holy Mysteries are not a matter of the priest making magical pronouncements over people or fulfilling some ethnic ritual.

The Mysteries are "liturgical," and this means "a gathering of the faithful," not "a ritual." An Orthodox wedding is a matter of the whole congregation (coming together) of the faithful in which the priest, as the ordained representative of the congregation, presides. The prayers are the prayers of the whole congregation, the "people of God," being led by their ordained presbyter. A wedding served only by the priest without the coming together of the congregation to bestow the prayers and benedictions of the Church jointly is not proper.. A priest ought not to serve any Holy Mystery or Liturgical service of the Church at which a portion of the faithful are excluded unless there is a seriously compelling reason.

According to Abba St Justin Popovich, Sunday is the proper day for marriage, the couple should have their marriage crowned at the Liturgy and, if they are both Orthodox, receive Communion together. This is why St Justin published the service of the Wedding Liturgy.

If we marry a couple on Saturday, it puts them in the position of spending their "first night" together on the eve of the Lord's Day, when all are called to be preparing for Communion, thus from the beginning, violating an essential meaning of marriage.[10] Decisions about such matters depend on how committed we are to maintaining basic Orthodox Christian perspectives.

LOVE: AN EVER EXPANDING CIRCLE

Marriage unites two people in a growing bond of love and makes them "one." But marriage involves more than the two people being united. The relationship between each individual and their family and friends will change – sometimes dramatically. In some instances, old friendships will slowly disappear. Family relationships will not disappear, however, and each partner in a marriage will acquire a new or "extended family."

From an Orthodox point of view, parents and family are important. An Orthodox couple planning to marry should work out their relationship with each other's parents and family before the marriage occurs. Much pain and difficulty can be avoided if there is a loving, harmonious relationship among the extended family on both sides.

The basis for this love and harmony is the love between husband and wife. A person is expected to "leave mother and father and cling" to one another. In reality, however, when a couple marries, each of them usually marries into a new family of in-laws.

How each spouse relates to the new "expanded family" can have a dramatic effect on the condition of the marriage. It should not always be this way, but it usually is, and this should be considered in the early stages of planning for a marriage. There are two special reasons for this in modern society.

First of all, we do not have the cultural and social support which existed in previous times and which controlled and helped shape our clan and tribal relationships. The old, clear, reliable standards of relationships have all but vanished in the modern hi-tech and highly mobile society. Our expectations should be reasonable and actually possible

The second problem is complex; marriages in which a young couple live at home and go directly from their family setting into marriage are sometimes problematic in our contemporary societies. This was not the case when the former cultural and social frameworks were stronger We now find that when two people have lived on their own for a while and "discovered themselves" before entering into marriage, the marriage tends to be stronger.

There are clear reasons for this, but it is an unfortunate situation. From a spiritual point of view, it is better if a person does not live alone, subjected to extra temptations from the passions. In that regard, it is better to live with one's family and leave home only when one marries, but in our society, this is only a vanished ideal, and experience suggests that it presents its own set of problems. When it does happen, each partner is more closely bound to his or her family, and too often, the other partner is not merely marrying the spouse, but he or she is marrying into the spouse's family. This may be the ideal, but it is not always positive.

It is important for the priest to discuss this with a couple who plans to marry. It is important for a couple to realise that their love will have to extend outward to their new relatives. Their love will, hopefully, expand beyond themselves and encompass the new extended family they are becoming part of.

Each partner should weigh his or her relationship with, and feelings toward, the extended family and realise the full implications it holds for their marriage. This matter should be examined and discussed frankly in the priest's preparatory discussions with the couple. We are referring here to an Orthodox Christian perspective while being aware that all these aspects are more difficult in contemporary societies. Even in the marriages of young people, spouses may have lived completely on their own for some time, as college students, for example.

Our children naturally expand the boundaries our love, and this extends to the grandparents of our children as well. Each partner should expect and understand the full implication of "sharing their love" with each other's family.[11] They should also understand the proper boundaries to this love sharing and firmly resolve that their love for each other and the marriage are their first and most dominant considerations. The couple should carefully resolve, ahead of time, questions about the expected limits. Marriage should outweigh all other relationships

There sometimes need to be clear boundaries to their parents' influence and involvement in their married life. They must put each other first and their marriage above every consideration while resolving to love and respect each other's parents and relatives. The priest, counselling a couple who desire to be married, should never neglect to discuss this important matter of relationships with the "extended family." Continued parental dependency on the part of one or both marriage partners is a frequent source of conflict and stress. It occurs predominantly with (but not exclusively among) individuals who have not lived away from home before marriage.

Over-dependency on parents and/or parental over-protectiveness can be a real destroyer of marriages if it is not recognized and dealt with effectively. Gentleness, compassion and understanding are necessary in these cases, but firmness and primary loyalty to the spouse are equally necessary.

ENDNOTES:

8. Man was not perfect in paradise. He was in a state of spiritual infancy and was supposed to grow and develop spiritually. In the fulness of time, he would have been given all things of the garden. By the "blessed condition of humanity in paradise," we mean his state of innocence and ongoing spiritual growth and development.

9. From a scientific point, "sex" used as a verb simply means "the exchange of genetic material." As a definition, it simply designates the difference betwenn one who produces eggs (ovo) and one who fertilises those eggs. We usually confuse "sex" with "gender," which is better understood as "sexuality."

10. It is easy to fall into a habit of being to routine and casual and disregard the actual meaning and implications of the sacraments. Even while expending far too much energy on external "culture wars."

11. This is ideal, but parents should not be allowed to interfere and, if nesecarry, firm boundaries need to be established.

APPENDIX 2
ORTHODOX CHRISTIAN MONASTICISM

[Some consider monastic tonsure to be a sacrament equal to marriage. Others deny this. Consequently, I am including it as an Appendix]

> *Monasticism is the barometer of Church life. The height or decline of the spiritual life of the Church in each epoch is defined by the conditions of monasticism in that period. Developing this concept, we realize that the relative height of the monastic ideal in each local Orthodox Church will show us how its children live and by what spirit they breathe at a given time.*[1]

This dictum is not new but has always been well understood in the Orthodox Christian Church, and it as been expressed from the depth of the Church's consciousness of Herself from ancient times.

Let us look briefly at monasticism and the essentials of the struggle toward the attainment of Christ's ideal.

It is said that when the embassy of Grand Prince Vladimir of Rus' arrived in Constantinople and attended the Divine Liturgy at the great church, the Cathedral of the Divine Wisdom, the ambassadors thought they had entered heaven. Indeed, Orthodox Christian divine worship is an image of heaven.

But ancient Rus' found an icon of heavenly things not only in the Divine Liturgy but in almost every aspect of the spiritual life of the Byzantines. One of the spiritual manifestations of the Orthodox Christian world which impressed itself most deeply upon the mind of Rus' was monasticism and the ascetic life.

2
THE MEANING OF ORTHODOX CHRISTIAN MONASTICISM, AND ITS SCRIPTURAL BASES

The monastic struggle is directed at nothing less than a spiritual life in the image of Adam before the fall. Our holy father, St John of Damascus, portrays this condition for us:

God our Father did not intend us to be burdened with care and troubled about many things, nor to take thought about or make provisions for our own life. But this finally became Adam's destiny. Before the fall, Adam and Eve were both naked and were not ashamed. For God meant that we should be thus free from passions. Yea, He meant us further to be free from care and to have but one work to perform: to sing, as do the angels, the praises of the Creator, and to delight in contemplation of Him, and to cast all our care on Him. This is what the prophet David proclaimed to us when he said, `cast thy care upon the Lord and He will sustain thee.' And again in the Gospels, Christ taught His disciples, `Take no thought for your life, what ye shall eat, nor for your body, what ye shall put on.' And further, `Seek ye first the Kingdom of God and all these things shall be added unto you.' And to Martha He said, `Martha, Martha, thou art care laden and troubled about many things: but one thing is needful; and Mary hath chosen that better part, which shall not be taken away from her,' meaning sitting at His feet and listening to His words.[2]

The monastic life, and the life of the hesychast especially, is an intensified striving toward these goals to which we are called and which are clearly and profoundly proclaimed in the Cherubic Hymn of the Divine Liturgy:

"Let us who mystically represent the Cherubim, and who chant the thrice-holy hymn to the Life-creating Trinity lay aside all earthly cares, that we may receive the King of all, Who now comes invisibly upborne by the angelic hosts."

To set aside all worldly cares and burdens and to strive for a spiritual life so free of passions that one is like unto an angel and so free from fleshly concerns that one's being is entirely occupied with the chanting of hymns to the Creator: this is the aim of the true monk. Monastic saints who have reached this goal of passionlessness, are called in Slavonic by a special appellative — *prepodobny* — which means "first likeness" or "first image," signifying one who has attained to the "original likeness" of Adam before the fall.

Monasticism is that channel which God has established in the Holy Church for the sake of those whom He has called to fulfil that higher calling, which Apostle Paul describes in the Bible:

"But to the unmarried and the widows, I declare that it is well [expedient and wholesome]³ for them to remain single even as I do" and again, "I desire to have you free from all anxiety and distressing care. The unmarried man is anxious about the things of the Lord, how he may please the Lord, but the married man is anxious about worldly matters, how he may please his wife. And he is drawn in diverging directions and he is distracted. And the unmarried woman is concerned about the things of the Lord, how she may be wholly consecrated in body and spirit: but the married woman has her cares in earthly affairs, how she may please her husband" (1Cor.7:8- 34).

Our Saviour Himself expresses this teaching in a parable: "...and there are eunuchs which have made themselves eunuchs for the sake of the kingdom of heaven. He who can understand this, let him understand it" (Mt.19:12). "From henceforth," our Saviour declares, "the kingdom of heaven suffers violence, and violent men take it by force." (Mt.11:12).

This violence is precisely the warfare against the passions, which are common to fallen man and which Satan uses in his struggle against our souls. This violence is the Unseen Warfare which St Nikodemos the Hagiorite describes.[4] The means of conducting the warfare, and the very essence of true Orthodox Christian monasticism, is hesychasm.

There is a certain basic vocabulary which is prerequisite to the under- standing of monasticism in particular, and the Orthodox Christian spiritual life in general.

3
HESYCHASM[5]

Assuming that you have really heard Him and been taught by Him, as all truth is in Jesus, strip yourselves of your former nature which characterized your previous manner of life and becomes corrupt through lusts and desires which spring from delusions; and be constantly in the spirit of your mind; and put on the new nature created in God's image, in true righteousness and holiness (Eph.4:21-24).

These words of the holy Apostle seem to be a most apt description of the essence of hesychasm; for hesychasm is a whole battle strategy against the passions of fallen nature which separate us from unity with our Creator. It is, in fact, the strategy which has come down to us from the ancient fathers, and thus we call it "patristic monasticism" and accept it as the criterion of Orthodox Christian monasticism. Essentially, hesychasm is a process of interior cleansing, of uprooting passions from within the depths of the soul, of purifying the heart, and of guarding the mind in order to prevent the re-entry of sinful thoughts which feed the passions and lead to actual sin. The practice of unceasing prayer — which the Scripture demands of us (1 Thes.5:17) is fulfilled by the use of the Jesus Prayer, "Lord Jesus Christ, Son of God, have mercy on me a sinner," developed under the guidance of an elder. The Jesus Prayer fulfilled in consultation with an elder is the central weapon in this interior struggle.

To understand this, we must look at the soul as a fallow field in which we are called to create a garden of salvation. This field is overgrown with tares (the passions). The sower, the parable says, sowed life-giving seeds. But some fell amongst the tares, and when they tried to grow up, they were choked off. Still, the Sower broadcasts these seeds all our lifetime, and when we see that the young sprouts are being choked off by the tares, we ought to understand that it is necessary to weed the garden of our soul so that the next season's planting can bear fruit.

This is interior work. It begins with the guarding of the mind so that thoughts will not interfere with our work in the garden.

5
GUARDING THE MIND

Guarding the mind is another practice that is best developed under the guidance of an elder. Sin, allowing passions to be aroused to the level of manifestation, most often enters the heart through the mind due to external suggestions. One must be ever alert to catch temptations as soon as they enter the mind so that they do not linger long enough to be committed either in thought or in deed (cf. Mt.5:27-28). To explain this more clearly: everyone knows, in a general sense, what is bad or what is good, or else one is learning. If a person is alert, he can quickly recognize that, say covetousness over some person or thing, has appeared in the mind.

Everyone is able to feel the initial thought growing toward jealousy and hatred. In order to grow, it must have our permission, it must have, as it were, a safe conduct pass to the heart. If the temptation is greedy covetousness, then the mind may be guarded by quickly beginning to repeat the troparion or kontakion to one of the holy Unmercenaries, or by mentally repeating the prayer, "Holy Martyr Panteleimon, pray for me." When this is done with faith, the saints hasten to the aid of the tempted one. When passions of the flesh are in- volved, the hymn "Virgin Theotokos, Rejoice" or "More Honourable than the Cherubim," when begun as soon as the temptation enters the mind is most effective, since the praises of the All-pure Virgin cannot co-habit with thoughts of defilement. The tempted one, however, chooses which will be the stronger of the two, the praises or the thoughts. In a word: everyone who is rational can train himself to be alert to the entry of destructive thoughts into the mind — though not, perhaps, infallibly in every case. Concerning how to take action to repel these thoughts, one ought to consult one's elder. The primary thing is intent.

It is easily possible to entertain the most foul thoughts while at the same moment repeating prayers. One must have the sincere intent to guard the mind fr om destr uctive thoughts, remembering, above all, that without Christ one can do nothing.

The mind is something like the door to the temple of the Holy Spirit.[6] The guard of the door is responsible for discerning whether "deliveries" to the temple are for its adornment or for its defilement. In this, the mind resembles a customs official who carefully searches through what is entering the country, rejecting what is harmful and admitting what is beneficial.

Thus, what enters the mind ought to be searched. Yet, the guard ought not to hope on his own strength, but rather, as a watch dog which barks to waken his master when an intruder enters, so one ought always to call on the Master to repulse the intruding temptation.

Everyone is able to practise this sort of guarding of the mind to one extent or another. Yet it is evident that the ability must be constantly built up and strengthened. In the end, the less that comes to the "door" the easier is the door to guard.

The more one withdraws from what is profane and distracting and enters into an environment of edifying things, the easier is the guarding of the mind (unless one falls into complacency, for Satan will instantly devise more subtle "deliveries"). This withdrawal from the spiritually destructive and advancing into the spiritually profitable and in to silence is the basis o f hesychasm.

If the body is the temple of the Holy Spirit, then what is there that can enter into it which is more edifying than that for which it is intended? It is most beneficial, then, to enter into the temple and, as a servant and worshipper, to clean out, to sweep, to dust and to purify the temple with repentance, confession, soul- searching, heeding the Holy

Scripture, and communicating the Holy Mysteries; and to strive most diligently in these tasks so that there will be a fulfilment of the temple, since the Holy Spirit does not co-habit with defilement, with the filth of pride, with darkness and with the foul odours of sinful thoughts. Either the one will increase and the other decrease, or the other will advance and the one withdraw. A "happy medium" will not be found, and no man is more foolishly deceived than the one who thinks that he has acquired the Holy Spirit not having first laboured long and obediently at the cleansing and purifying of the temple. Moreover, in this matter, one does not stand still: one is either on the way up or on the way down.

What enters the mind is either harmful or edifying. So the guarding of the mind depends upon intent and concept and is a much greater task than just sifting through parcels that arrive at the door. It begins with the free and open confession of every temptation and of every thought to the spiritual elder. To- gether with this is the cutting off of external enticements and replacing them with spiritual food: reading, as we said, sacred books, the Divine Scripture, constant prayer and participation in divine services, for these are the hoes and rakes of those who wish to create a garden of salvation in the soul. The finer work is done under obedience to an elder. Prayer is the stamina, the strength, the plough for every success will be seen to be a direct gift from God. Obedience is the harrow and the disk. Obedience is the crop insurance and the tending of the young sprouts once theybegin to grow. Obedience is the protective cultivation against the re-invasion of the tares.

Frequent communion of the Holy Mysteries is the ultimate weapon which burns up the tares so that the field of the soul can receive the seed and bear fruit. Nothing is attained without diligent struggle and whatever is attained is a gift of God's Grace in response to our volition.

6
WARFARE

This term is used to signify all the deceits, temptations and enticements which the Evil-one uses against us, whether seen or unseen, brazen or finely subtle. The deceits which Satan uses to rob us of our salvation are tailored to the individual character, for Satan is a psychologist with thousands of years of experience — moreover, he has largely shaped the psychological-emotional faculties of the fallen man. There may be brazen seductions, or deceits so subtle and so highly refined that the very intriguingness of the refinements leads to a fall. The vast experience of, and the revelations granted to our holy and God-bearing fathers, the ascetic fathers of the Holy Church, are indispensable to us in this respect. For the danger of spiritual delusion is ever-present in spiritual warfare. The guidance of an elder or spiritual father, and obedience to him are absolutely essential in the matter of spiritual warfare.

7
DELUSION

Spiritual delusion (Greek: *plani*; Slavonic: *prelest*) is the condition which results from succumbing to a spiritual deceit of the Evil-one, or from spiritual self-deceit. It is a state that may be attained by those who do not "contend lawfully" in the contest of spiritual war- fare. It can befall an individual or a whole group of people.

St Gregory of Sinai warns against spiritual delusion in the Philokalia,[7] and the twentieth century Church father, St Antony (Khrapovitsky), Metropolitan of Kiev, describes mass spiritual delusion to priests concerning holy confession:

Weak faith and carelessness are expressions of irreligiousness in people. But even a pious person is not immune to spiritual sickness if he does not have a wise guide — either a living person or a spiritual writer. This sickness is called spiritual delusion, or imagining oneself to be near to God and to the realm of the divine and supernatural. Even zealous ascetics in monasteries are sometimes subject to this delusion, but of course, laymen who are zealous in external struggle undergo it much more frequently. Surpassing their acquaintances in spiritual struggles of prayer and fasting, they imagine that they are seers of divine visions, or at least of dreams inspired by grace. In every event of their lives, they see special, intentional directions from God or their guardian angel. And then they start imagining that they are God's elect, and often try to foretell the future. The Holy Fathers armed themselves against nothing so fiercely as against this sickness — spiritual delusion. Spiritual delusion endangers a man's soul if it lurks in him alone; but it is dangerous and imperilling also for the whole of local church life; if society is seized in its grasp, if it makes its appearance anywhere as a spiritual epidemic and the life of a whole..." group of people becomes... "oriented entirely towards it.[8]

The words of St Antony of Kiev further illustrate our own era very well:

...anyone can pass himself off as a prophet, provided that he is not lazy, or ashamed to do so. No matter how much people are disappointed by his predictions, they will not cease believing in his (special) knowledge, but will explain the failure of the prophecy by their own lack of understanding. But the false prophets of Christ will have honour, glory and every possible gift heaped upon the man before . Everyone knows how destructive are the consequences of being Carried away by this `khlystism';[9] it begins Not all examples of mass spiritual delusion end up in depravity; some maintain very high examples of external morality. But Satan uses them to rob people of their salvation in other ways, as in the deceptive Ecumenical Movement, which appears so laudable on the surface, but which in fact is eroding faith and sound doctrine in every direction. The aim of spiritual delusion is to destroy the soul of one person, or of a whole group of people. Disobedience to the holy Church and her canons is the surest sign of mass spiritual delusion and false teachers.

8
ASCETICS:
SPIRITUAL ATHLETES

Apostle Paul often likens the Christian struggler to an athlete, and this is essentially the meaning of the term "ascetic:" one who trains and disciplines himself as in athletic training with struggles of prayer and fasting, and ends with shameless dissolution and unimaginable sexual Depravity.[10]

The athlete who has trained to contest for sensual pleasures has developed his spiritual and sensual "physique," his nervous system and muscular tone quite differently from one who has trained to contest for the crown of salvation. In the first instance, Satan has been the trainer.

Having drilled us in carnality and sensuality, he triggers certain immoral desires or passions within our hearts and souls by means of various suggestion s — various enticements, thoughts, direct seduction or mental tricks. However, a carnal minded person usually tempts himself. One who reads or watches pornography, for example, is in reality just committing spiritual suicide. If the carnal man desires to change to the godly contest, it is as if a runner desired to become a wrestler. It is necessary for him to completely rework his muscle tone, to completely retrain his nervous reactions, etc., for the running ability serves only that wrestler who, through cowardice, will desire to flee from his opponent. So also in the case of the struggle for moral perfection.

The passions, the former training, must be totally weeded out. The struggle begins with the open confession to the elder of all those things which serve to trigger the passions, and a careful avoidance of those things. Muscles which are not exercised become flabby and eventually atrophy. The guarding of the mind is a primary weapon, for the instant the triggering enticement enters the mind, it is still only a suggestion and can be cut off, gradually breaking down the training process. Carnal training can only be conquered by the successful weeding of the garden of the soul, for if the temptation no longer triggers a reaction — no longer finds a willing cooperation with passions or immoral desires — it will cease to become manifested as sin. Here again, nothing is attained without diligent struggle. Whoever struggles greatly with the most humility, comes nearest to the martyr's crown, having truly "crucified the flesh with its pas- sions" (Gal. 5:24). But note well that the Apostle warns:

"Except an athlete contend lawfully, he will not receive the crown even if he wins the race" (2Tm.2:5)

9
STRUGGLE (ASKESIS)

In its narrower sense, askesis (slav. podvig) is usually rendered "struggle." Its more complete, and spiritually correct, meaning is this: to contest lawfully as a spiritual athlete for the salvation of the soul, and for spiritual growth and development. It means that form of lawful spiritual contest which a Christian has embarked on as the means to "work out your own salvation with fear and trembling" (Phil.2: 12). For monastics, hesychasm is the primary struggle. It is the one taught by the an-cient fathers: it is the basis of patristic monasticism.

For the person living in the world, the struggle of raising a Christian family constitutes the major spiritual struggle — for there are but two channels of salvation: monasticism and marriage; and only a person especially called by God and sanctified to it will find an alternative. It is important to remember that obedience[11] is as much a prerequisite for the married person as for the monk.

10
ELDERSHIP

"Who shall ascend the hill of the Lord?" (Ps. 24:3)

In truth, the path of salvation is up a very steep mountain, and it is fraught with treacherous enemies and dangers of every sort. How difficult this path is was made plain by Christ Himself.

When He made known the difficulty of salvation, one of His disciple s asked in astonishment, "Who, then, can be saved?" "With man," our Saviour replied, "this is impossible" (Mt.19:25-26); and so it is, in a very real sense of the word — for man. But lest any despair, He continues, "But with God, all things are possible." For this reason, God has ordained that no man climb the mountain alone, having created the Church even before the creation of man.

Within the Church, moreover, God has called and placed guides — holy fathers who have left God-inspired writings, spiritual fathers and elders, so that even within the Church no one climbs up alone — indeed, no one can. A person who climbs a mountain alone, if he slips and falls, will have no one to sustain him, and so he will fall either to his death, or at least to critical injuries. If a group of climbers sets out on a strange mountain, they, being roped to-gether, may be able to uplift one another; yet if they climb without an experienced guide, they may all become lost or, taking a wrong direction, come to a dangerous precipice and the whole party may fall. But if the climbers set out as God decrees, under the leadership of an experienced guide who knows well the path, then they, being bound together with a line, will be able to hold a fallen co-climber, and the guide will set him upright on the path again. All together, they will be drawn up the mountain by the guide, helping and uplifting one another, fearing above all to disobey the guide, lest they fall into some precipice or knock a co-climber off the path and, the line becoming severed, one or both perish,

for "if the blind lead the blind, both shall fall into the ditch" (Mt.15:14). Let everyone see to it, therefore, that they are not led by the "blind," but by one who "sees."

This, in a simplistic way, is the nature of a monastery and of its elder. For the brotherhood of a monastery is bound together by the love of Christ God, and the love for God and neighbour. The greater the love, the stronger the bond and the more secure the life- line. By means of this love, if a brother falls, the other brothers sustain and uphold him, and the elder can rescue him and set him on the path again. For a person to perish under such circumstances, it is nec- essary for him wilfully to sever this bond, this climber's life-line, to cut himself off from the elder and from the brothers. In such a condition, he is certain to perish. As the brotherhood ascends in this way, the elder — the guide — draws the whole brotherhood upward and the brothers themselves, growing in love and obedience, draw one another upward, the stronger lifting the weaker, the faster climbers encouraging and speeding on the more sluggish by example and love.

Eldership is guiding climbers up the mountain of salvation, rescuing lost climbers, saving those injured by falls, and weeping over those who have perished — all the while, struggling to bring himself safely to the peak. And no one can do this unless Christ calls him to it and gives him the Grace to fulfil it.

Eldership is probably the most difficult struggle of Christian life. For in a very direct way, it entails the responsibility before God for human souls. It is also probably the very first "struggle," for the apostles bore the eldership of the entire Church and Christ Himself is the Great Elder and the complete pattern for eldership — first in Eden, on Sinai, and more clearly in the Incarnation.

Satan is the trainer of the athlete who wishes to contest for sensuality and perdition. God has given us the elder as the trainer of those who wish to contest for spirituality and salvation.

Eldership is a very great and deep subject and requires much care. We can best learn to understand it by reading the lives of the saints, and especially the patericons. God bestows spiritual gifts for eldership only upon those persons who have struggled for a long time in exceptional obedience, or upon some rare individuals whom He fore-knows. Such a person has been given sufficient control over his or her own passions to hear un- distractedly the most intimate thoughts of the spiritual children, and upon the greater elders, the Grace of discernment and even direct inspiration of the Holy Spirit has been bestowed.

The spiritual child, on the other hand, must be obedient to the elder, within the limits of spiritual life, and in all things which are lawful and not contrary to the faith or morals of the Church . The names teach t h e relationship: one who is still a child must obey and learn from one who is spiritually mature. The parent shepherds and nourishes and teaches the child, and the child who accepts all these benefits and makes the most profitable use of them has the truer understanding of the Scripture, and will surely save his soul.

ENDNOTES:

1. An old Orthodox Christian aphorism.
2. Exposition of the Orthodox Faith, ch. 11. The Nicene and Post Nicene Fathers, Vol.9, p.29-30, Eerdmans edition.
3. The quotation is from the "Amplified N.T." and the brackets provide the full meaning of the word used in the Greek.
4. His book titled Unseen Warfare is available in several languages.
5. (Literally: silence) Hesychasm is an active silence which may be variously defined as "inner work," or "inner peace." It is both and considerably more. The term itself reflects the inner peace which comes from obtaining control over the passions.
6. "What? know ye not that your body is the temple of the Holy Spirit which is in you, which ye have of God, and ye are not your own?" (1Cor.6:19); "Know ye not that ye are the temple of God, and that the Spirit of God dwelleth in you?" (1Cor.3:16).
7. see Writings From the Philokalia, Book 1, p. 80, Faber edition.
8. On Confession, translated by C. Birchall. Published by Holy Trinity Monastery, Jordanville, .Y., 1975.

9. Khlystism: the Khlysts were a Russian pentecostalist type sect that practised "ecstaticism." They began to think themselves holier than all other human beings. They ended up so deep in delusion that, in order to "defeat the flesh" many of the women cut off their breasts and many of the men castrated themselves, others gave themselves over completely to depravity. Rasputin was a member of this sect who chose the latter course.

10. Metropolitan Antony Khrapovitsky, op.cit.

11. Obedience is not "blind obedience." One is obliged to depart from an elder or a monastery in which heresy is being taught, or in which one's soul is endangered.

Printed in Great Britain
by Amazon

33833198R00086